Randeane Tetu is a Melchizedek Master and Karuna Reiki Master who has received national awards for writing. With blunt honesty, she chronicles actual experiences in what we know is true beyond ordinary beliefs and brings us into our deepest knowings, our most sacred feelings. This book brings us back to our own power to see our own beauty, to honor our own selves.

When the Trees Are Laughing

Et al is a collective of light beings which has the highest good of humankind and dear Mother Earth as its purpose. Listen to the words of these wise beings with opened eyes and opened ears and opened heart. Let them touch in you the feelings, the dreams, the knowings, waiting to be touched. Let them acknowledge with their love, the wisdom that is you.

Come to their words as to a lover for they speak of the Beloved.

When the Trees Are Laughing

By Randeane Tetu et al

ROWAN LAKE PUBLISHERS
Essex, Connecticut

When the Trees Are Laughing

By Randeane Tetu et al

Published by Rowan Lake Publishers
204 Westbrook Road, Essex, CT 06426

Printed in the United States of America
First Edition

ISBN: 1-928782-12-4
Library of Congress Catalog Card Number: 00-107635
$14.95

Other books by this author:

Merle's and Marilyn's Mink Ranch
Flying Horses, Secret Souls

For those who have told me,
"Stand in your truth."

Table of Contents

Gratitude and Appreciation

Thank you, those forces seen and unseen who have made this book.

Thank you, Mary Ann Libera, for working with me to make what I understand understandable to others. I find myself saying, "If Mary Ann understands it, I understand it."
Thank you, Ed Ziobron, for bringing the book to reality.
Thank you, Sandra Martz, for seeing what you saw in my first two books and for your advice on this one.
Thank you, Brian Jud, for your publishing direction.

Thank you, John for being here and taking care of things so I can "maintain the perfect fuddiness"
Buzhi for not editing this work
Katherine for your humor and lightness of being
Sharon Massoth, for your gifts of insight and encouragement
Rebecca Chase for telling me, when the book was started, "The heavens are singing."

Thank you for your guidance and confirmation in message circles,
Joyce Orcutt, Patricia Nelson, Al Ferency, Susan Ferency,
Barbara Dryden-Masse, Edna Adamson, Sarah Benson.

Thank you, Joyce Karpiej, Marilyn La Rosa, Peggy Goodrich, Edie La Barge, Deb Lees, Jim Coleman, Jim Shover, Jaime Cordova, Donna Gray Marino, Roz Einsohn, Doreen Armetta, John R. Jones, Deborah Kirk Welsh, Arlene Slater Stone.

Thank you, students who have taught me in all the classes I've taken and all the classes I teach.

Special thanks to these teachers, not only for the teachings, but, also for putting me among people who don't find this all that strange.

Aileen Raes, Reiki and Karuna Reiki
Sharon Massoth, Connecting with your Spirit Guides
Alton Kamadon, Melchizedek Method
Rebecca Chase, Andy Hahn, Dan Kindeleer, Guided Self-Healing
Anne Chandler, George Hoffman, Qigong
David Chandler, Tai chi

Much much gratitude to those who have hugged and blessed this book and sent it loving thoughts.

I trust you to accept these insights not as an autobiography, but as a glimpse of possibility. The details are given to help you recognize, in your own life, what people tell you, ways you are shown, ways to pay attention. If you recognize the details are not about me, the book is not about me, but about a way to be living in the consciousness of spirit, you will understand why so many examples of the personal are included and why I have dared to share them. If you read with judgment or to measure yourself or me, then have I missed my purpose. Not all of these messages are for you. The ones that are not are for someone else.

This book is a guide. It is not meant to replace the experience of working with a qualified teacher nor does it make claim to individual responses or experiences. As with any guide, you are the ultimate authority on how the information is used.

The author and publisher shall have neither liability nor responsibility to any person or entity with respect to any loss or damage caused, or alleged to be caused, directly or indirectly, by the information contained in this book. If you do not wish to be bound by the above, you may return this book to the publisher for a full refund.

Foreword

You are a beautiful instrument artfully playing the tune that we put forth. You are surrounded by music. There will be no paucity of tunes for you to play. Some will cause dancing; some will bring tears. All will move the very soul and open the heart to love.

What good is our music if there's not an instrument to play it? We thank you for listening. And we are grateful for your gift and your dedication. And we joyously applaud you in all of your endeavors. And we do so like your playfulness.

There's a lot going on in a lot of realms. Many dimensions show gratitude for your being who you are. It is good for you to know that, for you are our hope.

Through Rebecca Chase

You are making something from the realms of light accessible to the human. This feels like your life's work until now. And you want to offer it to others. It's so joyful to you – a way of being that has become essential. There's no other way to be than to listen.

It *is* to be footprints of light. That's right. You've written the language of universal mind and those who make it up and those who come closer to us to speak in their own language and give insights and learning so others can learn what they know.

You're a channel to others. When they speak to you, they are speaking through you to others. You draw lovely interesting guides. I'm getting the word anecdotal – human experience. We need the setting, the circumstance so people can understand it, so we become immersed.

I love sitting next to it (the book).

Through Sharon Massoth

You are working between the lines of the sublime and the intangible, the things that form beauty. The book is tangible but the feelings you get from it are intangible and also, sublime.

You are not just telling the feeling. You want the reader to follow the feeling. That's the power of it. This book has that energy – the intangible that is real – feels like healing energy. That's what we're talking about.

In order to fulfill the spiritual, the intangible, it takes work for the person to be pure. And you are a vehicle. You open your eyes. You open your heart so you can see, you can feel, and you can transmit that spiritual force.

When you open your mouth, the spiritual words come out of your mouth so those who will hear will be close to god. They hear something that makes them close to god. They say, Oh, yes. And they are thankful.

Jaime Cordova

That which I hold sacred.

All that I thought I was doing was making notes to later remind myself this really happened. Then, as if in a dream at the edges of sleep, the book proposed itself. Only as I began to understand how to put this book together did I see its greater purpose and recognize how my life's events have brought me to create it. If I'd known where I was going, I don't know if I would have come to this place of opening to you that which I hold sacred.

Compiling these notes on scraps of paper into readable form, I question, "Who am I to tell you this?" and hear, "Who am I *not* to tell you this? To keep to myself what is given to the world?"

And so, as these words are for you, with much appreciation and thanks, I offer **When the Trees are Laughing…**

I began writing some years ago as a way to remember what I knew as a child – what it was like to climb down onto a wooden chair into the square deep hole with roots of trees sticking out from the sides, where grandpa and my father were extending the driveway, or what shadows the clothes on the clothesline made dance on the lawn. And from there, I began writing stories.

For me, writing a story is like coming upon a woodland creature that for a few magical moments allows me to follow it home. I must be respectful and quiet and trust it to lead me and not impose myself upon it. And then I hear a line or see a place or a person. And I write it down. And as I write, I see something more about that person or place or suddenly know who said that line of dialogue and what he will say next. I don't know where that character or that story is going, but as I listen and let myself see without interfering, I find out. And I write it down and, as it completes itself, I give thanks because I know these stories are through me, not of me.

Because I'm a writer and because this is how the process of writing works for me, I write down the experiences of dreams and words that come to me while I'm walking. In summer of 1998, I was writing a book of short stories, and, as I began to hear words that were not for stories, I wrote them down, as well.

This book is written as a journal, the recording of a journey, showing how I discovered as I went along. Were it not a journal, you wouldn't be getting the details, dates, and notes on what I was doing at the time. I've recorded this so later I could be sure it really happened and I didn't make it up.

One night in a dream, an angel walked before me in darkness and left lighted footsteps for me to follow. My intent in this book is not only to bring to you what I was writing down, but also to show you the footsteps, for each of us has a place in which spirit communicates and these experiences of awareness are available to each of us.

This book is meant to give you the experience of following a guide to gain the confidence to do this yourself.

I show you the simple messages as well as the profound because so often we have insights we dismiss when they seem ordinary. I had to learn to notice the small messages such as "Go ahead and drink tea." It was when I gave attention to each experience and stopped waiting for the grand ones that I allowed this fuller appreciation to bring me more.

I'm asked to share what I think is personal to me because it is personal to you. Remember, as you read, the book is speaking through me. When you read, "You are loved," it is spoken to you. Because "Someone who reads this book will respond to these words, also," I expose my doubts, my humanness. Not from a place of my small self, but from a place of deep trust in the knowing that knows more than I do and sees beyond what I see, I present these private moments, reminders of that which you already know.

This is the book of what happens when I listen, when I set aside time to pay attention. This is the book that gives credit to the beings of the realms of light who've written with me and guided me in the making of the stories, and in the making of this book. This is how I understand it now. And yet, I know, there's more.

You don't have to have certain beliefs to experience the intent of this book. You don't have to have any training. Whatever metaphor you use for where these writings come from – guides, higher self, angels, mother/father god, Great Spirit, divine within – is appropriate.

You'll discover several bringers-of-words as I discovered them. One of them, Shilogh, comes to me as a Native American guide and then, partway through the book, lets me know he dons this costume because he knows I will accept him as a guide in this costume.

Read, not with your beliefs, but with your knowing. As you listen to the words, let the ones you don't need go past, like water in a stream. They are for someone else. Flow from one page to another; you'll know the ones that are for you. What doesn't apply today may apply another day.

Or, open to any page and let the words guide you for this day. The sequence in which you read is the perfect sequence. In this way, you create the book for you.

Take to your heart what resonates. And whatever questions are not answered, ask yourself. And listen. For as you tune into your own brilliance and light, you invite others into theirs.

Dates and setting show that this didn't come all at once, that guidance responds as we listen, and that the more we honor the wisdom by paying attention, the more it comes. The journal format honors my original intent – to remind me this really happened.

You can understand the messages of the book without the explanation, but here's a key to what I was doing.

To give you a sense of what's going on,
what I'm saying is in *italics*;
what I'm receiving is in the body type;
what I'm seeing is indented on both sides.

A hyphenated date entry (e.g., November 16-17) – Reminds me that the message came in the night. I do a lot of taking notes at night between sleepings. Before I started doing this, I'd remember in the morning that I'd had a sparkling experience, but I wouldn't remember what it was. Now I have pen and paper near my pillow and write in the dark.

Dreaming asleep – Means I was asleep and dreaming and woke to write down what I remembered. Dreams are sacred messages from spirit. I choose not to watch television or film because when I do, I don't dream my own dreams.

~ **Dreaming awake** – Shows I was awake, but at the edge of sleep, nearly dreaming, drifting between sleep or just waking.

~ – Shows the symbol I use on my dream papers for dreaming awake – same as above – in that state between sleep and waking or just before waking. At the beginning of the book I note "~dreaming awake" and let it go when I think you've caught on.

A single-date entry (e.g., November 17) – Indicates awake and up in the world. Often the words would come as I sat with first tea. Often I would chant or meditate and then hear words. Often I would ask, "Is there a message?" or some other question.

Writing room – Indicates where I was, physically. I teach fall and spring semesters, and during the summer go to the room I rent for writing every day and begin writing before I'm fully awake. This room has space to dance when dance is part of my writing. The ritual of chanting, meditating, or dancing helps clear my energy field and invites the writings. When I first rented this space, my mom gave me the figure of an angel which I put on the wall. I dreamed her name was Merope, looked it up in the Oxford English Dictionary, and found Merop means "Good words or good speech."

Invoking – Invites source energies for the highest good and acknowledges those energies which work for me, with me, and through me, for the highest good of the collective.

Chanting – Brings the worlds close. I chant the Karuna Reiki symbols for as long as seems appropriate. Singing works as well. Sarah Benson tells us our singing nourishes the angels.

Meditating – Soothes the conscious, doubting mind and allows the suspension of disbelief; excludes the chatter of this world and allows the thinning of the veil between worlds.

Muscle testing – Allows us to access deepest wisdom by using the body and energy fields around it. The energy field of the body signals a yes or no answer. I use muscle testing as a way to confirm that what I'm receiving is accurate, from highest wisdom, for the highest good. I used this procedure to determine what was and was not to be included in the book.

Tap, knock, ting, and other noises – Bring my attention to the importance of what I'm hearing or confirm that it is correct. I've included the sound in parentheses where it seems appropriate.

Goosebumps or energy sparkles – Come to let me know the connection with spirit and deep truth.

Tears – Come as my soul recognizes my soul.

For someone – Means the words have been delivered to a specific person and are included here so they reach others who are wanting to know them as true.

Namaste – Means "the divine in me recognizes the divine in you" and is used to show respect, reverence. "Namaste" is my way of honoring those I sense or feel or see or hear. It can be spoken or motioned with the palms of the hands pressed together and a slight bow of the head.

Cosmic christ consciousness – Is not limited to a particular set of beliefs but represents the mastery of love on all planes. I call his representation Jesus at first and later, Sananda.

Suggestions

During the time of these writings I was meditating daily, walking often, and drinking lots of water. I was not eating refined sugar, watching TV, listening to radio, or reading newspapers.

"If you would but turn off the noises that are external, the ways others interpret your world for you, then would you hear the language of your own soul, your own soul song."

I don't believe these are requirements but they seem to have helped me stay focussed. We're always getting messages, talking to ourselves, and not listening to what we say. But guidance is available when we attend.

You might develop your own ritual time and place to let spirit know you're listening, but also, be open to what comes at all times. Notice the worlds around you. For me it is noises and taps. For you, it may be colors or melodies or a feeling. Allow the universe to speak to you, touch you in whatever it is you notice. And notice when it does.

As you develop your own rituals, you'll notice what does and doesn't work for you. Your willingness to increase what works and decrease what doesn't work, honors and respects the process, allowing a clear path for energies of guidance. Whether you receive images or words or feelings or knowings, honor what comes for you without wasting focus wishing for what comes for others.

These things help my practice of listening. You might notice which of them help you and compose a list of your own. This is just a guide.

Spend time outside in nature each day, especially with trees
Dance
Engage in gentle exercise
Chant and sing
Meditate
Get quiet and listen
Ask a question and be open to the answer
Give yourself time
Suspend your disbelief
Allow your imagination
Keep pen and paper near the bed "for when your dreams wake you to
    write in the night"
Write down your dreams
Accept your awareness
Resist the inclination to edit or discredit what you receive
Avoid talking about your insights with those who may discredit
    your experience
Allow others their beliefs
Trust your own knowing
Be joyous in who you are
Allow your doubts and set them aside
Play
Breathe
Appreciate
Teach others to see their worth
Write what you see or hear or know so later you're sure it happened.

CHAPTER ONE

Be kind. To yourself and others.

February 26, 1998

Once upon a time, a beautiful child was born. She kicked her feet and waved her fists and discovered her new body. Made of light, she knew who she was and where she came from. The light within her shone and affected others. Then she was expected to take care of herself and got caught up in this world. And that child is each of us.

And tonight we remember that we chose to come here to learn. And we thank others for the lessons they teach us, even when the lessons are hard. Even when we don't think we want to learn them. We release blaming others for the lessons they teach, realizing that others fulfill their purposes in teaching.

We release with forgiveness any bitterness against others or ourselves. We release with gratitude old habits that no longer serve us, that stand in the way of our becoming who we are.

As we honor the connection between heaven and earth, we remember who we are. We recognize ourselves as holy, lights of the divine.

March 23, 1998 afternoon

Anything on death?

Death is a transformation, a change only, from one state of health to another state of health. People fear death but don't need to. It is nothing. It is a change you are ready for, a cave that narrows to a fine point and then the light.

On living?

Live each day every moment. As if death is coming. This is what death is for. Not to fear. To appreciate living. Congratulate yourself.

On what?

On trusting, believing. It isn't easy to do. To release yourself to trust, faith. Living. Put in seeds. Water them. They grow. This is what the earth teaches. (knock to my left) Whatever you want to grow. Plant the seed. (Now I see the Christ-Buddha seated cross-legged doing teaching and hear a knock.)

Nap following: dreaming asleep

I'm shown three ways. I try all three. First is closest to their way, last closest to our way. I learn from each. I say yes. Whatever you prefer. I understand. I understand completely in the dream – each way. Valuable to receive information. Golden coppery light over all during dream.

June 15, 1998
A message for one in the hospital near the edge of this life and the next

Be of good cheer. All is well. The road is easier than it has been. Trust yourself. Trust the universe. You are not without helpers. You are not without guidance. May your way be easy and your spirit light. May all be well with you. When you are tired, sleep. When you are ready, wake. The best way to help yourself is to not get in your way. Take what you need to nourish yourself. We are here to guide/help you. As you replenish yourself, we rejoice. As we can serve you, we rejoice. Think not that you take away from anyone else what it is that you can use. It is for you. Energy, guidance, wisdom, breath. It is for you. You know how to use it. Allow it to be used.

Everything starts now and everything can change. You start now, each moment creating the next one. What's in the past is gone. The future is how you make it. Starting now. We are with you. We are ready.

You decide in each moment. We help you manifest. A decision is necessary for us to act. We act only with your permission.

Don't fret about this. Let it be easy. Let it be light. Let people/beings you have always known take care of you now. Let patience be your guide. Let ease be your lesson. It is done.

Thank you. Is that all/everything?

Keep heart. You are deeply loved. There is nothing you must do. There is nothing you must work at to receive this love. It is for you. You may take it. Enough.

Thank you.

You're welcome.

I love you, dear ones.

And we love you.

Is this message as you want it?

Yes. It is complete.

I hope I'm hearing you right.

You are.

I worry that I'm just using words I've heard.

Well, why do you think we put them there? (I'm amused and smiling.) Of course you are.

June 19, 1998
For the husband of the woman in the hospital

She's gone through the veil of illusion. It will be difficult for her to come back. She can do it, though. She can do it if she wants to. If she tries. But you can't make her that decision. You can't make yourself the failure if she doesn't. This is not about you. This is only about her.

June 19, 1998 morning, writing room
For someone

There is much love here for you. You walk in good intention and the way is made clear. Gather not thoughts about furtive questionings and, instead, gather knowings. Recognize that parts of what you do come from here, and gather energy from these parts of you that know.

Your minds are busy questioning in the way of this world as if answers come with justification. Not necessarily. That's what makes it awkward at first to trust what you are knowing. Reasons abide in the busyness of worldly events and sometimes cover/hide knowing.

Trust without reason, without thought, without groping, and what has been furtive about your doubting will be shown as clarity. That is, the doubts you have not recognized will be cleared, not necessary.

Walk in goodness that comes to you out of your goodness. Accept the clear stream of energy that comes to/for you. Beware turning it aside because you don't understand it – in the way of "able to explain it" because the small fears make you question. As you learn to accept without having to "know," you will know.

Be patient. Be gentle. Be aware. In your awareness you … (I see a person with light all around – as if to show, your awareness is a pool of light that others may step into) … step into light. This takes nothing away from you and adds nothing to you. But it can add to others.

Be kind. To yourself and to others. Be not jealous or guarded, but generous with what is yours to give. What is yours is needed/valuable. Recognize it. Honor it. And give it away. There is more. There is more and more.

Don't be afraid and hold it. It is light. It cannot be held. As it shines forth, it renews itself, again and again and again. The giving away of itself makes place for the giving of more.

Think not that this means the light is not for you. You are lighted as you use it. Energy never being spent but always being used.

We are complete in your using the light. It is here to use. You are the gift of using it. Be aware and do not hesitate because of trying to hold it. Always pass it on. It is always there for you.

Make romp and play on this glorious day in your world.

We are with you. Be at peace. Fare thee well. Abide. (I see a circle of faces above me, leaning altogether to shout!) We love you. You're doing well.

June 20, 1998 morning, writing room. (Writing stories which later become a writer's guide, I wrote down the first couple sentences and then thought I'd lost the rest of the story because I was moving around.)

Your connection is not that fragile. Your connection is sturdy. Give it weight. Pull on it. It doesn't break. It doesn't come undone. Give it time, as well.

We like the chanting.

You don't *have* to teach the world.* You don't even have to teach one person. Make yourself at peace.

How do I set up the connection?

It will come. It is important. You have the gentleness of spirit that people respond to. Take the advice you gave for someone else. Don't fight it. Learn how to know it so you accept yourself without hesitation, without reservation.

This writing, thank you, comes so easily. It seems I've been training for it writing stories. Stories come to me something like this.

Yes. Learning that the right words are important. Though stories are your own fabrication of what it is you know put into words for others to draw meaning from/understand. Trust that we come from the same source. These voices and the voices for stories. When people understand this, they will listen to the stories newly – with interest. The connection will be made. You'll see.

The connection between this new channeling and the stories?

Yes. In print. On the media. People will be made aware so as to expand your teaching/influence. So that people will listen and know truth in themselves.

Am I just hearing what I want to hear?

You are *also* hearing what you want to hear.

I am not making it up?

We are making it up.

Thank you.

Enough. Now we begin (again, on the story).

*At qigong class some months ago, Anne Chandler asked us to get quiet, picture a computer screen, and ask for a message from the universe. My message was, "You are meant to teach the world."

June 25, 1998 writing room 9:30-10:00 in the morning
> I sit with amethyst and quartz for Reiki grid (a pattern of crystals which holds energies for specific healing purposes). I chant and my arms move as in dance. I feel to my right a beautiful presence which I can make into Jesus, Mary, sky goddess, angel, but don't need to. I'm sobbing and tearful. I beam energy and sing again. Then this message:

I bring a message of good tidings and love for brethren and for nations which all are one. The same light which shines from one shines from many. It is not lost forgotten deep. It is floating coming to awareness. It is sparkly essence of touch, of voice, of being.

When two people or more share this sparkle essence, there is more than would be from the two. You understand this – how energy creates energy and life creates life and breath creates breath. Do your part in creating breath, Randeane, as you are doing. All else comes to you. You do not need to chase after. You need to let things come.

Aren't I getting better?

You are getting better, yes. Happiest girl on earth. We're here to guide you, remind you, help where you forget.

You are so welcome here. I love it that you come, that you stay and I sometimes see you, hear you, feel you in tears.

It is not a shabby thing you do to be on earth, walk in lightness. It is a high calling. The priestess in you, the goddess, expressing. Don't, then, take lightly the importance you have as you choose things lightly for your good and the good of others. Sing. We like the song. And, yes, you're getting better. Call us whenever you want us. We will come.

If not earthshaking news, we always have something to say. Dreams, yes. Keep using dreams as a way to reach us and your world. Influence for highest good. You are right to choose not fear as you did last night. This builds not fear around you. This builds safety and trust that others notice and respect. We protect you. Turn your thought/mind/talent to other things. You are manifesting now what is drawn toward you. Intend now what will come.

Health
Well-being
Safety
Creativity
Space
Play
Breath
Song
Joy
Delight
Desire
Passion
Stories
Freedom
Trust
Awareness
Faith

Thankfulness
I choose to teach
I choose to recognize others as they would ask to be
I choose solitude when I need it
I choose wealth beyond daring
I choose this place, this time, to be called upon and to respond
I gather energy for well-doing
I thank you and the heavenly ones
Amen. Be it so.
Thank you.

Do you think we are done?

I think so.

We are not

I am listening.

No. You're thinking.

That, too.

Walk calmly. Do what you like. Eat what you like. We will help change your beliefs. Thrive on what you take into your body and beam your well-being to others. You are impatient. Afraid to run out of paper. Then get more paper.

I have some.

See? What need to fear? Be calm, assured. You are making changes. You can make changes. Take it easy and be loved. Amen.

Thank you.

Enough. Fare thee well. Prosper. Goodspeed.

June 27, 1998

I believe that I'm to be writing.

Yes. We have that belief also.

And that I'm to be writing this specific book at this time.

Very much so. It's why we're helping in a more "visible" way just now. Do you like it?

Very much so. Thank you. I worry or fret that this book will mean my others are taken less seriously.

Then start a new line. The world being as it is, your other books might be compared. To the good or to the detriment. Rejoice in the writing. Let the world do what it will. That isn't yours to ponder. We like the dance, yes. And the drumming sometime if you like.

Chapter Two

Honor your gift.

June 29, 1998 afternoon nap – home, waking

Anything for the people I'll see this evening?

There is much love for you here. As you gather to minister to each other, you minister the universe. Not your planet only, but worlds beyond. As you give and receive willingly with each other, you transmute this willingness to worlds. It is not then, kept among you, but goes beyond. Pick somewhere it is needed. It is there. Or let yourself be open and it is received where it is needed. Either way. Fine. Thank you. Those of us working with you establish connection and work with joy. Work is not the word we mean but the word you understand. It is our joy to be with you and to accept what you offer. We learn with your learning. Think not that you must know all. Now. It is not given unto you to know all but to play with each step to rejoice in light. To understand – light and knowing are not the same. That light is you always and knowing returns in pieces you can handle – make use of. You need know nothing to be light. Don't let your light be murky by contemplating what you know or don't know. By comparing with others or your own wanting. But let your light be clear as it is at this time that you come together with each other. Carry yourself in trust that is yours while you are here, outward from here. Others do not need to know who you be or what you do to benefit from this purpose of yours – sharing light, reminding others of their light.

We are grateful as you come together. We are grateful as you leave. (At this point, I see us turning away from the inward circle to expand on light beaming outward through us and around us.)
So be it. All is well. Fare thee well. Abide and prosper.

Thank you. Amen. Enough.

We are not greedy for your time?

No. I am greedy for your time.

We have none. It doesn't matter. We have plenty. Don't count it.

Thank you.

Be at ease.

June 30,1998 morning, awake, (listening to a drumming tape at writing room I find myself in a field. A medicine man comes to the edge of the woods. I see him in a headdress and leggings of fur/fluff feathery white.)

You are loved. You are wanted. You are real.

Take what you need. Ignore the rest. All is well. All is balanced. Eat hearty. Be not afraid of foods. Let them help you. They are from the earth. You need not reject the earth. Rather use it. Be here. Be it. Revel. Gather grains and fruits and sunlight. Know your true self in these as you did when you were a child. The questions you wrestle with, put down. Let them not touch you – as when you were a child. Let the sunshine touch you. The earth. The air. The trees. Struggle not. Resist not. That is not for you.

Be like water, flowing with lights on it. Softly. Easily. Alive. All is well. You don't need to change things for this to be so. Soy. Fine. Good foods. Fine. You worry about them. Not fine. What matters is that you accept them as the nourishment they are.

Thank you, Great Wise Father. Be welcome again.

(Lightning as I open my eyes and huge rolling thunder.)

July 2, 1998 home, outside, afternoon, meditate

This morning, the medicine man, who calls himself Shilogh, is near my face with a straw, drawing out toxins. Now he stands at the edge of the woods and shakes his rattle.

He dances. He comes into the clearing, shaking his rattle and dancing, whirling, calling up to sky, down to earth, a cleansing ritual.

Now I am lying and he dances around me. Grit comes from his dancing onto my face, lips, breath. I see this from out here, looking on, but I feel the grit. Now he brushes it off with feathers like a duster.

Brushes down my body.

Walks solemnly around me clockwise, stepping on toes first, then whole foot. Carrying feathers upward in two hands under his chin.

Now a wider circle, dancing again, chasing out what he's drawn out, whisking it away in wider circles.

Now he sits, arms on knees and rests, looking at me, watching. Shakes duster yet again outside circle.

He watches until nightfall. I still lie in the center. When it is dark, he leaves back into the forest. I can wake up when I'm ready. I signal namaste to him in the forest and come back to here on a lawn chair outside.

What if I doubt?

You don't have to believe for it to work. That is taken care of.

July 3-4, 1998 ~ dreaming awake
For someone

Be not discouraged. How do your guides get you to the right places if not by directing you from the wrong places? Keep in your minds your image firm. Keep it firm. Don't waver. In wavering you make it more difficult to draw toward you. Keep firm your image and your feeling of it that you already have it. And don't despair. When you despair, you take away from the image your strength. Your strength is needed for the image to manifest. We do not do this without you. Cannot act without your decision. Remember free will. You have free will to manifest only what you choose.

Why this, situation then? Contrast. And getting you to the right place of knowing you decide what to bring to you. Contrast shows what you don't want. Now use that contrast to state firmly, with conviction, what you do want to bring it to you. Dwell not on what it is you don't want because then that is what you bring to you.

You do not exclude it from your vibration by not wanting it, but draw it toward you – whatever you picture. Therefore, picture not what you don't want. Replace it with what you do want and picture that with vibrancy. With assurance it is coming. This is law of attraction. Carefully now, with mindfulness, attract what it is you do want.
Peace. Love. Greetings. Fare thee well. Prosper. Abide.

Enough?

Enough. Love to you all. Many blessings.

Thank you.

Thank you. You relay our message well.

July 3-4, 1998 ~ dreaming awake
(I see Shilogh and bow to the ground.)

Do not bow to me. Rather love me.

Thank you for the healing.

It is accomplished. (He raises his head and hands to Great Being. The headdress of soft feathers tips with him as his head tips.) Make thanks to the Great One. Works through me.

(In the clearing, I tip my head back, open my arms to the sky.) *Thank you Great Being for healing, for making me whole. This and other blessings I appreciate. Thank you. Thank you for Reiki, (method of relaxation and stress reduction which allows natural healing to take place) for symbols and feeling of connected.*

You're welcome. Our great pleasure in you. (Rain soft drops fall around me in the clearing. Shilogh bows his head to me, farewell, disappears backwards into the forest. I stand in the rain, smelling earth, trees. Small animals come to the edge of the forest, watching. A deer. A bear. An octopus. Now here I hear the birds.)

July 7-8, 1998 morning, waking
(Shilogh stands as if, You would speak with me? I see the forest and him there.)

Good morning, beautiful one.

Good morning. You are doing well.

Thank you. Thank you for coming, for dancing me, for helping, for leading on my path.

This is what I do. I walk with pleasure and with joy to help you.

What is needed now?

Comfort. Relax. Use energy wisely and well. Not in jitters or wasted motion.

I think I'm getting better at that.

You are. You are.

Others have to work it out. Not you. They have to sort things out. Discover things. You stand back and allow it. Your part is to observe. Let it go.

Thank you.

There is more. Walk lightly with yourself. Shake your rattle. Dance. Be easy. All is well. Keep yourself. Do not berate yourself for yesterday (didn't buy a chair). These things happen to good purpose. You will see all is well. Good that you recognize, discern between your action and the guidance of your guides. (I thanked my guides and blamed myself.) Yes. As is proper. Take responsibility for yourself. Not blame. The mirror is a good thing. In that room. Good. Reflects you and the light. (He starts dancing now, head down, head back, rattle shaking. Dances backwards into forest.)

Namaste.

July 10, 1998

Please help me write fabulous stories that people will enjoy and learn from and recognize as themselves, to be helpful and uplifting. Please use me as a vehicle for wisdom, understanding, love, upliftment, encouragement. And thank you for taking such loving care of me.
Yes. Today I'm taking care of the vehicle. Sitting under the tree.

This is good and very good. We appreciate your attention. We appreciate your loving yourself.

When someone else tells you, it's easier to do, even when you know, yourself, you should.

Yes. That's why we do that. Because people don't listen to themselves.

I think that's why we have children. So we listen to ourselves as we speak truth to them.

It is so. Very wise. Don't you want to gambol in this weather?

Yes. But first I'll take out the clothes.

Yes, but then please gambol. Enough for now. Prosper. Abide. Fare thee well.

Thank you.

You're welcome.

July 11, 1998 morning after dance and chanting
(I see him at the edge of the forest. Two lines of feathers down from his shoulders like wings.)

Shilogh. Welcome beautiful warrior guide.

Welcome beautiful warrior.
We recognize your divine intent. We see your wings. We watch your angel self lift off to hug others, to bring encouragement, uplift. It is clear to us what you are doing even if you don't yet recognize it. You are beginning to. As you feed others, you feed yourself. As you love others,

you love yourself. As you pay attention to the needs of others, you pay attention to the needs of self. You are an extension of divine grace, divine love, divine well-being. You hear the messages of good intent. It is no surprise that bear has come to you to hold the hammock. * You bear good tidings to this world. People are seeing light in you. Do not hide that light. At home, especially. Be not afraid and hide the light. Much progress is being made when you let a little shine. Be willing to up the amperage. Be willing to trust lighting up dark corners. The more light your house holds, the better it reflects you. Yes, we have sent you the mirror you want that you may see reflected the light that you are, that you bring, that you bear. At your own speed, when you are ready, test that the light can be stronger. You are making now of your place above stairs a lighthouse. For others to steer by. Your voice, also, a light. Your voice calling energies that you can use. Called me (he preens a little, dances to show off). Calls others. Keep calling. You may be surprised at the answers, the visitors, the expression. It is well. Do your papers now. We've finished.

Thank you.

Prosper. Abide. Farewell.

*At Sharon Massoth's class, Sharon asked us to go into meditation. Others go deeply, but I stay pretty shallow. Sharon says, "How did you do?" I admit I was still pretty busy in my mind. I felt I was creating safe space for others. "That's exactly what you *were* doing," she says. "Let us create space for you now. You tell us what you see."

I see a runway of light up to a hammock. She urges me to get in, but I can't mold to it, relax. Jesus, Mary, Kwan Yin, Grizzly Bear prepare the hammock. But I'm all elbows, all angly, not relaxing. I realize I'm afraid I'll take advantage of accepting care. Sharon's guide tells me that I won't. "Relax into it for the world." At this, I fit into the hammock and seem to become Jesus with children around me. I'm teaching, caring. And now it's hard to come back. But the hammock is still there for me as I return here.

"Let other people help you," Sharon says. "You'll be pulling in greater abundance. There's been a shift – a real shift. You'll keep getting ripples of energy to remind you who you are and to connect with your divine self."

July 11, 1998 afternoon under a tree

> Very tall people in a semi-circle behind me are making a chant, sprinkling it around. They're not focussed on me but on each other, laughing, talking. And now, directly in front of me, a man flies in on a cushion. I've met him before in meditation. His name today is Dunna. We bow to each other. He likes the carpet that is hanging on the clothesline. Like my cushion, he signals.

A flying carpet. Yes. (We bow.) *May we hold communion with each other?*

Yes.

> Light beams connect me with him. Crown, heart, third eye, throat. Underscored with green. I hear almost singing, almost music. Someone creeps forward on the path around the corner of the house – I feel a tug between my wings – to leave me something. As we'd leave a May basket. Dunna has orange-red around him and sits with eyes closed, palms toward me. Underneath his cushion, a cloud of white light that holds it. I feel a tug in my upper left arm.

> Be still and listen. Be still and listen. Listen to the quiet. (Behind me, tall beings toss blossoms up on the air. I am being nourished by Dunna as a mother would nourish with milk.)
> Accept yourself as divine. Accept your life as charmed. Understand you can do no wrong. You can only choose directions. Four directions and many more. You clear directions when you meditate and when you move the chi (energy in the body). Skin brushing (brushing the body with natural bristle brush) is good for moving chi.

> Jesus is here, to my left. Mary and Kwan Yin, to my right. The bear puts his paw on Dunna's cushion but then removes it.
> I am becoming a blossom. I am being nourished with light. I am becoming translucent. A white flower. Lily. I smell a scent

of blossoms. I drink in the energy. I flow it back to Dunna, see it move along the beams which circle back.

I see the form of a tiara or headdress. Now he hooks up all the chakras. I begin to glow like a lamp. Oh, Jesus and Mary and Kwan Yin are beaming me with their hands.

I see that I'm being fueled like a car, being fueled with energy. I start to feel my third eye, buzzy and soft.

My intention is to be a vehicle for God. (I become aware of a situation I'm resolving.)

What is the danger here?

The danger of forgetting who you really are.

But as I improve the light, won't things happen naturally?

They may. Or you may have to push them. Are you ready for the push?

I feel a lot of resistance.

We can help with that. ... This will become clear. Remember holding on when you're down off the water skis, and how easy to let go. And someone picks you up.

Yes. I remember.

We'll pick you up when you let go. ... As much of it as you choose. You choose. And that's how it will be. (Oh. They start disconnecting the hoses/beams from me. Dunna is ready to leave. The others turn to bow heads to him. Behind me, tall beings run off.)

Show me how it can be done.

We will show you. (Dunna recedes backwards. Others *Namaste* and I do. I feel uncomfortable. I guess that I'm supposed to. I look for the gift that's been left.)

July 12, 1998 early morning, first thing

> Out the kitchen window, I could see Buzhi, the cat, where she
> often sits on the crossbar of the clothesline pole, but when I
> opened the door, she leaped off the crosspiece and took flight as
> an owl with a length-of-my-arms wingspan. The owl landed
> on a tree limb, waited while the real Buzhi came up the path,
> and then flew into the woods.

July 14, 1998

Maybe later we'll have a message for ... (I name someone)?

We are ready.

All is well. Know that you are loved. Know that you are necessary for
the balance of the planet/universe.

Your light is needed in dark corners where you live. Your light is
needed shining outward to others.

Be not afraid to come close to your needing. Be not afraid to ask for
help. Our help and the help of others. For you are helping us and others
with your presence.

Value not lightly what it is you bring to the world. It is much. And
doubt not yourself in your ways of bringing it. There are no mistakes.
You can do no wrong. **Impossible**. There is boundless light and much
learning. If you have chosen a hard path/way for your learning,
congratulate yourself on your courage, your bravery, your fortitude. You
teach others as you learn.

You are a talented teacher though you think not to value yourself so.

It is time to be selfish in the best sense. That is, listen unto what the
self needs and would like. Listen well. Be it peace? It will be peace. Be it
love? It will be love.

Struggle not against the self who is here at this time, this gift of
divine form, manifestation, body. Rather find what you need/like in it
and provide. As you decide your needs to be here, we can provide what
will help you have comfort.

State what you need not as lack, but as what is coming to you, because,
truly, what you envision and hold in your thought, you draw (they are

making clear draw, as a picture, and draw, as in pulling) to you. Therefore, state only what you want to come to you, so we may bring it, joyfully.

You are much loved and much needed here. We appreciate you. Much love and many blessings.

Faith, Fare thee well, Abide, and Prosper

All greeting from your loved ones. It is time to be full of health and full of well-being. Let any other thoughts go past, and capture in your silken net the prosperity and well-being you seek.

July 18, 1998 I ride along with Sharon Massoth to a class she'll teach at the Wainwright House. As she drives, she channels this for me from her guide:

> "It is right to whisper the truth you know to yourself, but then, let it become a roar. Whisper your dreams. Then let them become a roar."

> *Is this about the book?* (At this time I didn't realize it was *this* book.)

> "Yes. Intent means everything. Your intent is to help others, do good works in the world. We recognize this intent – very honorable. Those in spirit are part of your team. Many work with you already and will continue to help you unfold.
> "Keep honoring your intent and help will be there. Intent means everything in terms of creative potential.
> "You are a divine, breathing arm of god and you need to know many forces move that arm. You are receiving an incredible amount of inspiration already; this will increase exponentially more as you increase your willingness to be a channel of your divine self.
> "So come close to us as we whisper to you the beauty that you are in the world, and let us adore you again and again. Let us shine forth our love to you and our acceptance because you are a part of the world plan of transformation. You are a light bearer.
> "So accept today this responsibility as never before and know

that as you take it seriously, you will find how much fun it will be.

"Accept our congratulations on the acceptance you have in your heart to our words. Many blessings."

(I'm laughing now at how bold I was to ask Sharon to speak slowly so I could write this word for word. And how glad I am that she did.)

July 19, 1998
For someone

Honor your gift to write.
Allow it space and time.
Your headaches will ease – it's a conflict.
You have a gift in writing. Tell us what it is you know and can say so beautifully.
(Goosebumps big time.)

CHAPTER THREE

This is but a seed of the great tree.

July 23, 1998 morning as I drive to the writing room
Message for someone

Be of good cheer. All is well. Delight awaits. Whether the answers come now soon or in time more than that, the answers will be good answers. Be not impatient, fearful for your small little job. Be aware, instead, of your larger job, your higher intent and know that all is well.

You are given a time to test your own strength of purpose, your own value, your own worth. Meddle not with setting things to contain your small vision when you are given opportunity to create your large vision. See your own worth, your own daring to be great. In this opportunity, see your limitless ability to draw close to your greatness.

These are loving times which demand of you loving actions.

Your higher good is drawing near. Battle not to maintain what is in your desire to stay put. Rather see your ability to expand. Lift your head up and see the stars. Mock not that ye be not mocked.

July 26-27, 1998 (I was writing down a dream when this came through for someone)

Focus on being present. Being a light for those around you. Unfocus on that which you don't like or don't want or you draw it to you.

You are here to be present, draw good things, spread your light which is the light of your divine self. So be it.

Prosper. Abide. Fare thee well.

July 27, 1998
For someone

You are fine. All awaits you. Pleasant is the journey and pleasant is the stay and the coming home is joyous. Be not afraid of coming home to your loved ones. You have been missed and there will be rejoicing. You will be glad for what you've done, where you've helped. Your influence is felt. Grieve not at the leaving of your friends. For truly, you are coming home.

Is this soon?

Not soon yet.

Thank you.

It's a jewel.

What is?

This lifetime walking among mortals.
Prosper. Joy. And abide.

July 28, 1998, during a nap, morning, writing room

> "The maiden's fire. There she is, how she looks." (I look and see the moon. It seems a doorway for the maiden into other realms.) But the cat is her mode of getting back in. "Oh, look at the poor girl. She wants to be inside," (she says to bring herself back in) lets the cat in to let herself in.

*Some messages, like this one, mean nothing to me at the time. On April 30, 2000, Barbara Dryden-Masse noticed the cat pin I wear on my jacket and told me I have a feminine presence who is closely linked with the cat working with me and helping with the book.

July 29, 1998
Message to the student

You are here not only as a student, but also as a teacher. Your light reminds others of their light.

As you learn, you change. You become more clear. What once you thought hidden becomes revealed. What once you thought mystery, you now understand.

Think not, then, that you are here to learn reading or psychology or any label. But that you are here to learn and grow/change. The changes you make in yourself help others make changes also.

All learning is remembering what you already know. In this class let us, then, have joyous remembering.

Let us put aside the excuses and reasons for not remembering our power, our light, our joy,

      and come into our strengths

      and come into our gifts

with great freedom, with great wanting.

Let us set aside the fear of being as great as we are and learn to use our greatness for the good of ourselves and others.
So be it.
Abide. Good Strength. Good Learning.

July 30-31, 1998 morning ~ dreaming awake

Good morning, Shilogh. I love you.

I love you. I have a message.

Thank you.

Be strong. Be sturdy. Don't let things distract you from your purpose, your calling. Be like the warrior with one-point focus and see how the other points converge to that focus. You are good at this. You have been training. Use what you know. Don't waste it, but use it to keep focus now on this new intent, this broader perspective which will then/now brighten all else/all that you do. It is for you to use so don't lose sight of that. It is easy if/when you keep it in sight. And you can do this easily. Be aware that you do it already. The meditation is good. The dance is good. The song is good. Drumming also. You don't need to do it yourself for drumming to help you. The tape is fine. A good answer. You can do it/ use it/journey by yourself – with helpers, of course. (He stands a little straighter, chest out, chin up to show he means himself, especially.)

(I smile.) *Yes. Thank you.*

There is much to be done and much you will accomplish. Notice the little things. Appreciate them now for soon you are great/you recognize/come into your greatness and things are fast. Very fast. You love it. You have trained for this also. (I think travel.) Yes. And travel. All travel. You will see. You have done well learning to fly. Now you fly. All is well.

Thank you.

It is a word you use a lot. We understand it. You are very welcome. You are loved. From here we see your good works (goosebumps lots) and appreciate it all.

Thank you. For it.

Thank you. Sincerely. Abide.

We work well together. Play well together. (I think of chanting when I get to the writing room, but also start silently now.) This is good.

(Shilogh has on the long rows of feather headdress now and moves his head in sort of jerks to make the feathers ripple. Vague impression of others behind and around him but not too close. He has his own space at the edge of the forest, now in a sunbeam spotlight as if on stage. He crosses his arms in front to look worthy of the spotlight, then winks to the side at me.)

August 6, 1998 morning, chant
Message for someone

Yes. He must be patient. What you have been wanting to do all your life is coming toward you. Keep your well-being now. Keep yourself as the changes which are coming at first feel awkward. They will, in time, feel joyous. Doubt not your role in this joyous expansion. You have been practicing/rehearsing to be here/comfortable here. Honor the sense in you that wakens you in the night. Treat it not as happenstance. You are a remarkable couple who work together in joy. Think not that any one thing you have done or are doing is wasted. It is meant that you are here in this moment with all other moments of your feelings and knowings. That is, what you have learned counts.

Embrace it as you step forward now in your readiness, in your eagerness to expand/go forward, make a difference to others as well as yourselves. Check for yourself if you haven't felt some change, some difference in the tone of things, the light of things.

Am I making this up?

No, sweet one. We are telling you so you can tell him. He is more comfortable being in the know.

Yes. This is true.

The light continues to grow. Randeane has said and it is true, "I want to shine my light." And we can act on that. Be careful what you say. This is not arbitrary or to be taken superficially. A large part of what you do is let her shine, protect her so she can, allow space so she can. This continues, growing more important, even, as you will see. Ask yourself if you accept this. Always there is choice. This choice opens into fullness, wholeness as you go forward with each other, expanding light. Fullness abounds. Well-being abounds. Uncover dark spots that hesitate and let them be filled with light. We are joyous at this fulmination of many years.

Be aware. Prosperity abounds. Wellness abounds. All is well. Abide. Prosper. Faith and Charity.

Thank you.

Thank *you.*

Is this a message I deliver?

If you like. At a time you like. It is fine either way. You asked.

Yes. Thank you.

He does like to be in the know.

Right.

Enough.

August 7, 1998 morning, meditation, chant

Any messages? For whom? For someone.

All is well. Think not to tease yourself with what you should or should not do. Do what you will with joy. Hold yourself not back from things you like, but embrace them with your wanting. All is well. Your body accepts what you give it with love. What is not given with love, it resists. Choose foods that give you a feeling of wellness and don't "should" yourself about them. Your body is comfortable doing what it's doing but will learn a new way if you teach it. Will respond a new way to the new thoughts you feed it. Thoughts are the important food. Know all is well and feed your body thoughts you would like to draw to you. Dwell not on what you wouldn't like or that comes to you also.

Say to yourself, "I am already good at doing it this way. I choose to try a different way and be just as good at that. I choose − a decision carries much energy and power.

Healing attunement (Reiki) would be fine for removing unconscious blocks to what you are wanting.

That sounds like me talking.

It is. But we tell you what to say. (Comment: I love it.)

Okay. Thank you. I guess I've been saying it right, then.

Oh, yes. We are happy to work with you on healing and on talking about it clearly.

Thank you.

Take advantage of what is helpful. You don't need to do it alone. Gentle exercise walking, stretching, would help you appreciate your body as it changes. Feel Good.

Put aside worry which can make you hungry. Fill your self with love that people feel for you.

Much is being accomplished. You are very loved. So be it.
Aware. Faith. Abide.
Enough.

August 8, 1998 writing room

I'd like to be free of toxins. And I'd like to drink tea.

Drink tea.

I'd like to feel good about it.

Drink tea and feel good about it. It is all right. Your body is doing extremely well. This can not influence it.

Thank you.

(As I open my eyes, the tea service I've set out for angels is the first thing I see.)

Oh! Yes! The angels drink tea.

August 10, 1998 writing room, with tea first thing

Let's see what we have today.

You're doing very well. Don't hesitate to congratulate yourself. We join with our approval. (Toast, ovation, standing.)

Thank you. It's beautiful to be writing with you. I love it.

Take time to appreciate what you've done. Take it easy. Relax. Enjoy. The stay with (someone I'll visit) is important. She loves you more than she can tell you, admires you more than you know. This, in fact, is what makes her irritable, cranky, at times. That she perceives you as completing yourself in ways she is not yet. She will. Through these times she will come to those times. All is well. It is not her nature to be brittle. Her nature to be complete. And she knows this, knows she can be more. Why she chose a challenging school. She may even think it's the name, but, really, it is the challenge. The stretch it will bring for her – intuitive as well as intellectual. She has already started the path of the spirit. Encourage her to be not hard on herself.

There are no wrong choices. Whatever she chooses, commit to it with full heart with full appreciation.

Discouragement is a sign for change. But not always action. Often change in attitude. It matters not the circumstances. She knows this.

But attitude always matters. It is because from the mind – the attitude – come the reality, the manifestation. This is true. And she struggles most often from not recognizing this.

Look how long it's taking me to learn.

Yes. Our beautiful slow learner. You must learn everything carefully and forget and re-learn in order to make it yours. Now will be easier. Because you trust us. Now things go quickly because you are not off pushing against every thing to see how far it goes. Wasted energy. Now is easier as you stay with your connection. We like tea. Stop fighting that. That is just one person's generalized opinion (that it's not good for me) – useful, not exact.

Thank you for clarification.

This one is like you in that she accepts no one else's truth until she has experienced it. But is hampered by intellect at times she could let go. She sees she wants to be right and hasn't yet seen she wants to be happy. When she learns that the highest good is keeping herself in spiritual alignment with source energy, she will be happy and let being right go. It doesn't matter. We don't care about being right because there is no wrong she can do. There is no wrong others can do to her. She will know this. But will come to it her own way. As you have done. Testing, doubting. It is all good.

May I read her this?

Of course. Isn't that why we are phrasing it?

Thank you.

Whatever she does at school, they will know she's there. Her friend, we adore.

I do, too.

He is the proper amount of question and answer at this point. They both grow. He reflects her state of being. She can learn from that. That is, whatever in him she would change, change the corresponding part in herself. Use this genuine reflection of her for her own improvement rather than for his. For as she changes, she reflects him and he will learn from her his own reflection. It cannot fail. Watch it happen. We don't say this in play. (jest) You say jest?

I would.

Jest. Good word. Like gesture.

Um. More like jester.

Jester. One who jests. Gesture. One who Gests.

Now, you jest.

Yes. Much love.
Abide, Faith, Hope and Peace

Thank you.

All is well.

August 14, 1998 morning, chant 7:30 or so at writing room
Snow Leopard

I bring you love. I bring you light. Camp will be grand. Conference illuminating.* You are doing well short-term. Think long-term now. Think coming into your power. Travelling in body, as well as spirit, to people who need to hear you. Churches. Temples. Great halls of learning. Think global. Translation will be there wherever you travel. Countries wait for you. This/our message not only for your country but all peoples. They will love you where you go. They will listen. They will remember. This is but a seed of the great tree you become. A very good seed, strong seed, and now a seedling. Feel yourself as the seedling holding power and majesty of the whole great tree. Because soon, as your roots strengthen, your top shoots up. You turn in breezes. This is good. So much good nutrients, however, you cannot stay small, a small tree. You push outward and up and become larger. Still a tree. More visible. People notice. Not so apt to be cut over with the lawn mower. You see?

Yes.

And now you feel your bark rough and strong. Still you move with the breeze, not try to stop it, but also solid, firm in connectedness. Enjoy this now as it comes. Release the seedling, the cover of the seed. Become the great tree whom people notice and come to for peace and rest and hope.

Free your self from your part to become this. Revel. You will not become proud. Fear not that aspect. You understand well in terms of humans and in terms of spirit. (Bells chime out from church.)

We are ready. We are all ready, including you. This is beautiful, delicious, enchanting. You love it.

Okay.

Have tea or breakfast.

Okay. Thank you.

Abide. Peace. Fare Thee Well.

*We're going to camp for a week. After that, I'll attend Melchizedek Method workshop.

August 16, 1998 at camp
I find the message from August 14 in my camp bag. Morning.

How beautiful, Snow Leopard. Thank you. (goosebumps)

And we mean it, (I hear.) (Good thing I write these down. Once hearing it, reading it, is not enough to remember and really feel it. Oh, I know. I'm so excited with the message coming in that I miss the *message!*)

August 19, 1998 at camp in the morning

> I meet my divine self, who holds me in her lap as if she is a mother. This reminds me that I heard, "I am the mother of all mothers," in a dream some years ago.
> My whole body is bathed in light with starry sparkles.

Let not the opinion of others disturb you, cause you to feel you must act a certain way. Release yourself from their expectations. *But they are mine!* And also yours. There is importance in what you speak. Trust yourself to say just the right thing without saying so much that you put people off. Yes, continue discussion this morning – that's fine. More good will come.

Enough?

Enough if you come again soon. We miss you if you don't.

And I miss you. I love you.

We love you. Good night.

Good night? (It's morning.)

We know.
Abide. Faith. Love. Harmony.

August 21, 1998 near dark at camp
(Shilogh, feathers down his back, raises and lowers his head, arms out.)

You like this place.

I like its songs. Its sense of itself despite people around, Yes. I like the water. The lake. The sun going into it, the trees. I like the fishes. The bear who is my brother. Here on the island is peace despite disruption (of people). It is a good sense of self, of being used wisely. Forgiving and content. Happy to bring wellness to so many. I like this ground. (He stamps it on the pine needles, looks up the trees at the sky.) It is good, good place. Good people. Respect. More than elsewhere. Respect for each other. Air moving briskly and clearing off moods, cleansing. Renewing. Recharging energy as it lulls, lulls, lulls. (He sinks to sitting posture. Cross-legged. I see a campfire.) Happy. (In the cheery light, he takes out a pipe. Lights it with a coal. Puffs. Content. Nodding.)

Good night.

August 23, 1998 back from camp, chant at writing room

Is there any message?

With whom would you speak?

With everyone. A message in general. For the world.

Accept peace. Live peace within you that peace may manifest without. Live free from fear which draws to you distress, disruption of peace and joy. Live free of doubt which causes unbalance.

For you

This conference – fine. One caution: Beware of being overly influenced by others. Bring it home to yourself. Check it with yourself. You know how to use what you learn and how to release the influence of those around you. Each person translates to his or her own experience. If the translation does not seem pure, go after it yourself. Go to the source now that you have the information. Phrase the question from *your* experience and hear the answer in your experience. This means not to doubt, but only to confirm in your terms. For your growth and good. People are of good intent. That is sure. Their intent draws for you what you can use and what you can clarify. This is good.

Back to the world

Peace is ready to break through. A gathering of peace thought is imminent and peace manifests. Create for yourself a place where peace may gather, undisturbed, clear, shining. And people will find that place. And people will create that place in themselves. And others find that place, are drawn to that place. Their wanting of that place for themselves draws it to them. Becomes their priority.

When they are willing, nothing can shake that. When they are firm within themselves, resolved, peace surrounds them. Influences others. You see how this works. One person starting/deciding – creates a space others step into, take home to themselves. Create so that others step into. This is for the world. Her time now is for peace. One person matters. One person can do much. You will see this is so.

Be the person. We are with you. All is well. Sleep in peace. Dream in peace. This is how it is when you create worlds/the world.

Honor yourself for being peace. Shudder not when you are not peace. And come back to it, new. Newly resolved. Newly intent. By that you know yourself. When to change/adjust. When to keep straight ahead. All is well. You cannot fail. Only become richer and richer (fuller). So it is.

Enough.

Abide. Good peace. Well-being.

August 24-25, 1998 5:30 morning

(Waking from a dream about my brother who is living in the spirit world. I see/hear him say, "Hi, Sis.")

Hi, kid. I hear the Grandmothers are taking care of you. I've always thought you died to be with Grandma. You missed her so.

That's partly true. But the world was so heavy. Like a horse lying down, I had trouble breathing it. I came in to stir things up. Out of complacency.

Well, I'd say you did that. They've never recovered.

They're not supposed to recover. Change/adapt/go on. Not go back. Or what I did was wasted.

I'm learning to trust a divine plan and so understand what you say.

Yes, trust the universe. . . . It was when you released to the highest good – stopped trying to be in charge of making things right – that everything changed.

Oh, yes. A friend of mine, is newly on the spirit side of living. If you would, please greet her as my brother. You are so good with gifts. If it's appropriate would you give her a gift? Tell her that I love her? That I admire her bravery and courage – that I recognize she held on for the rest of us. So we would be all right in letting her go. She is so beautiful. I could see her wings here. See her in the blue and yellow "wedding garment" meeting her angels. Ready to meet the divine.

(Now I speak directly to her and she answers.)

You have a voice now. If you would use my channel, you may.

I am extremely loved here. It is as I knew it would be. I am resting. So tired and yet the word is energized. Resting to be full/filled with sparkling energy that is different than the heaviness/the feeling of having weight that you have there. It is a feeling I was coming to know before crossing. Because of it, waking in the world on earth was an unwelcome surprise at times. (She names her husband) is fine. He is steady though he doesn't know it. He has found his strength through this in a way he hadn't before. It is because in doing for others he gives his all. You have seen, it is hard to accept for himself the Reiki. He wants to give it. To others. Not take for himself. In this, he will let others help *him* as he has been learning to do. In asking help, receiving help for me.

Tell him to accept it now for him. This will be important. Complete the circuit. Love going out coming in. If he needs to, at first, accept it in my name, that, also, is fine. So long as he learns people are needy to love him now, to express their love. This is the situation for it.

I'm going to go now. I love you, too. You are a special person. Doing God's work. Thank you.

Thank you. Thank you.

All is well.

Yes. Amen.

August 25, 1998 dance, chant, beginning the fall semester

Gather. Clouds. Roll them into bundles. It is the way. Climb down the stone steps into darkness and look up. See the stars in daylight how they sparkle.

See the truth in dreams how it shines.
All is well. Early peace.

Early peace. Good morning.

My divine self is already here – tall and beautiful, sitting on a stone bench.

I step forward and become her. Now I am tall. Magnificent. Regal. Gracious and graceful. I move slowly – there is so much of me. My head moves slowly. Even my flowing garments, slowly.

I feel like a Disney character. Floaty. All-smiling. Benign. Breeze makes curls of water around the edge of the garden across some walking stones. I lift, drift just above the stones.

I see a woodchuck, a squirrel, watching me. Teal colors, bends of light zing around like sparkle. Ah. The hammock. I'm walking to the hammock* between two trees. Just the right height. I get in, give my weight to the hammock. Drift on the sturdy breeze. Kwan Yin and Jesus and the bear and Mary – No, Mary couldn't come – stand in light a little off. I motion/invite them close. They look in at me. They touch the hammock edges. A cat gets in with me. Buzhi. Curls by my side.

Before I open my eyes, I see gentle rolling French countryside in front of me. Smell hay/grass. Now I see my divine self/me in the hammock with the cat. Headdress not disturbed.
Oh. I don't have to get up yet. They'll rock me.
I come back slowly. Divine self floats back to the stone bench, cat in her lap. I hug her.

*hammock that Jesus, Mary, Kwan Yin, Bear set for me in an earlier meditation

CHAPTER FOUR

Your lovingness shines from you.

August 25-26, 1998

If there's any message, I'll take it.

You are loved. Completely loved. Doubt not that this is so. Even as you are loving us, we are loving you. But more. Bigger. In bigger streams than you can imagine is our joy. In your recognition of your divine connection/connectedness. Sacred – this is what sacred is, means. The part that recognizes god. Is god and sees itself as extension of god. As the hand recognizes its use to the body and performs with willingness, openness, trust, that its action is appropriate to serve the entire.

You are recognizing in these moments you call time your physical beingness relationship with Source.

Stop trying to make our words/think them – and just write them. They will come. Better without your trying.

You are loved. We are sincere. Understand how needed you are. Not as an entity separate from us/spirit/source, but as an entity *of* spirit/source. The hand serves the whole body; the entity serves the whole source. And is, by it, served.

Imagine now, the hand has consciousness, free will, to serve with the rest of the body. For the good of all. You will see how great our joy at the conscious choice of Yes!

You will see, also, how those happy fingers dance.

"You are the living, breathing, arm of the divine, the hand that holds the pen." This is true. Doubt not.

Be assured that as you choose/accept to be guided, you will be guided. Yes. You are anyway, but how much more that you are willing. Think of a student who is not willing to learn and one who is. Think of the joy of discovering with the one who is. Also, we know, with the other. You take the time, the encouragement to lower the resistance and make it happen.

But, yes, you're right. There is a supreme joy and giving with one already eager to learn. I see what you mean.
Yes. Please help me be the learner who is willing. Please remind me, as you just did, when I get in my own way. Of course, I want to be the best I can be. With enthusiasm.

Your enthusiasm is splendid. Causes light. We are one. In agreement. In purpose. We work/play together well. Call us if you need us. We are always here.

All is well. (I see them – two – lift me into their arms. Large people with flowing sleeves on their flowing garments – more like cotton than silk.)

August 26, 1998

(Shilogh is seated cross-legged at the edge of the forest. He lifts a long-stem pipe to offer to me. Yes. I puff it, take it as an invitation to sit to his right. Fire burning – small, comfort.)

Great opportunity comes to you. Already under way. Be sharp. Keep your purpose. Hold your focus. Remember dreams you have. Remember you said, "I am ready." It all comes to you now. It can't wait, is already in motion.

Fear not for security. State your mind. Higher purpose than you is working out the details. Money comes. Fame comes. Well-being abounds with you in the center of it. This conference (Melchizedek Method workshop) changes your perspective still further, enhances your ability. Draw to you all that is good. Leave the rest – with your blessing. All is well. The way is made smooth for your next assignment. Step into greatness as stepping into the lake at evening/dusk. Walking into it to meet it, be surrounded. Be part of what it is – lake. To be lake. Dive into it in noontime heat and feel it satisfy your wanting. The lake is here for you. Hold not yourself from it. Revel. In full confidence. It is yours. What you have prepared for, are ready for. Enjoy. Delight. Revel. Dance. Yes, dance.

> He stands to dance with me, a sort of stamping bop that becomes more open, free, wild, as we wriggle our hands above our heads. The sky is nighttime now. I'm not sure if it was before – no, daylight. Sparks leap upward. We leap upward. We sound voice from our very essence of being. His feathers seem alive as we whirl. They surround me.
>
> Someone is dancing with us now in reckless abandon. Many dancing with us now, unfettered, exuberant, living. Someone raises his head, tips backward to the stars and lets his voice ring out in tone. Now I see us subside. A pleasant form of drowsy, we lie on blankets as on magic carpets that drift us to other worlds.

Many thanks, Shilogh, my brother.

Many blessings, little sister. (He sits by the campfire, keeping watch as others sleep. I come here.)

August 31-September 1, 1998 morning waking
(As I was remembering what to write from a dream, I think Shilogh wanted to come in.)

Would you like to come in now? Sorry to make you wait.

There is no waiting here. Only for you, who didn't have the message sooner.

You are loved, sweet one, with all our hearts. There is nothing like this that you know yet there on earth though you will. Soon more and more people will know this – what my people know. And then the world will shine, sparkle, twinkle like a star. You will see it is so. It is enough for now. Get up and going in your time.

September 3, 1998 someone calls to say their cat is lost.

> I put on music and dance. I see the cat. She is showing me she's
> scared and it's dark. She's lost, and I dance her home. She goes
> through darkness into light.
> (Later a neighbor calls to say she's found the cat, but she's not
> living in this world.)

I hear their cat:

> Mommy guy daddy guy. I tried to make it home but I couldn't.
> Please don't be angry at me. Because I had to go. Haven't met anyone
> here yet, but it's nice. (I tell her to look for our former cat and ask her to
> come.)

Now in a dream September 5-6, 1998

> Your cat. She's back at her house, not your house. And now she
> knows where she is. She can leap and play – she's showing me –
> like a kitten. She will come to earth again, she thinks and bring
> love again sometime. She doesn't know when. But she liked her
> time with you. She would do it again. She says the fur wasn't
> her fault. Wasn't on purpose. She tried to be good. She's running
> off now. She doesn't seem to be alone. I sense others around. It
> seems a full-size house or the impression of one, though I can't
> quite see it. Not a small house like for a cat.
> She's blowing hearts like bubbles back over her shoulder. If you
> find a little puffy heart you'll know it's from her.

September 14, 1998 morning
For someone

> You are of the chosen people and therefore, why does god not take
> care of you? Have you not thought that you are chosen as a teacher? Of
> others. As a teacher for yourself?
> You think the way should be made clear. Why not this and why not
> this? But it is for *you* to make the way clear home. For this have you been
> given opportunity to be here. For this have you called on your
> circumstances.

Judge not god and others in what they do for you. Do you for others and give thanks. Then will you see the clear path, the way made clear, the gem it is yours to have and keep and shine around you, reflecting god's light.

Be not discouraged as you plan your activities, but throw your thought into the universe and see how it comes back to you, guiding, changing, beckoning, and so…

You are very loved. Show what you have to others. Show not what you think you lack.

Speak gratitude for what you have to god that may be filled in all around what you would draw to you. Focus on abundance. Release lack.

So be it.

Farewell. Abide.

September 17-18, 1998 dreaming asleep

Someone who taught at the college, and is now living in the spirit world hands me a manual he's prepared for me to teach the writing workshop.* It's 1:30. People are coming in for the workshop. Some go right into meditation before I've given any instructions. I haven't seen this manual before so assume the man who gave it to me will help me through it. But he goes to a different room to teach a different class, confident that I'll do fine.

Two people I've seen before come in a back door. Everyone seems far away in a circle. I invite them closer and one wise guy brings himself right in front of me. We all adjust.

I have some words to say about writing in joy. My voice seems so loud to me. Now we start on the colored workbook and I'm seeing the pages for the first time, figuring out what to do. The participants go along with me.

I feel very good about the man's confidence in me, and willing to follow along the colored workbook though, if I'd known,

I would have come earlier to preview it.

*I'm to present a writing workshop tomorrow.

(September 18, 1998 I thought I knew what I would teach at a Writing Memoirs workshop tomorrow, September 19. But when I go to the writing room, I sit at my desk and write a meditation. Only later do I notice the sychronicity with the dream.)

A meditation for writing:

We write well when we admit writing is bigger than any capacity of ours alone and are willingly led by the writing.
Let's do the workshop the way I write. Let's take ourselves to a safe place and get quiet, and without expectations, see what happens.
Close your eyes. Get comfortable.
Breathe in…breathe out.
Quiet yourself so you can see and listen.
Breathe in clear energy for writing. Breathe out concerns, worries, tension, any thoughts that limit you to this time and place.
And as you breathe, realize it's morning . . . and you are a child.
You are a child in the house where you lived as a child.
Wake up in your room there.
See how the light comes into the room if it does.
See the patterns it makes on the wall or ceiling.
Sense who else is in the house as you are waking up.
Where are the others? What are they doing?
And now, step into your day.
Pull on some clothes and go to the kitchen.
Look around at the morning.
Someone comes into the kitchen or someone is already there, and you realize this is a day you remember as special.
In the morning or the afternoon or the evening of this day, something happens that makes you recall it with clarity. It could be a large something or a small something.

Don't work at this. Just let the day present something.

Staying in that place and in that day of childhood, invite the child you were to use your pen and say something about that day on paper.

Stay out of the child's way and allow whatever words come to get onto the paper.

Without judgment, without control, even without opening your eyes very much, stay in that place and allow the child to write.

Anything.

Let's do that now.

And when the child has said what she'd like, recognize her as a wonderful child, honor her for who she is and what she remembers or makes up.

Say good-bye in whatever way seems appropriate.

And bring yourself gently back to this safe place in this time.

September 18, 1998

You are very loved. Yes. You are very comforted. The program you think of for tomorrow (meditation for the workshop) will be excellent. Excellent. How could it be other with the people who are to be there there and us helping you? Yes, as you have thought/seen, people will come to hear you as they come to hear other authors, but with different purpose. With purpose of upliftment, taking on their angelhood, taking on their wings as you lift them to higher perspective with your words, with our guidance. It will be so. Has already begun. Has already completed and will manifest. Judge not whether this is right for you, what you want. It is what you came here for and thus, appropriate. Do you not see that you do this already on a smaller scale. The same will you do for many and many. The energy will come for you to do this. Your body is adjusting now. Feel the tired times and enjoy them. We are working. Sleep enough to feel comfortable and do not worry if you miss writing down the dream. Take comfort in the *feeling* it was wonderful. It was.

As you step ahead, things will come to you that you need. People. Situations. Places. The footsteps of light are for you. (In a dream, an angel walked ahead of me, making footsteps of light for me to follow.)

To light your way and make it easy. Do not tire yourself on little things. Tire yourself on big things. For you are big and growing bigger as, yes, you grow into the tall self you dreamed. It is for this you are working. We will provide. Care about things as you do. Look for the gifts you like to give – tangible – and recognize the gifts you give without thinking. Yes. The way is smooth, no? Because you have asked and changed your heart place on the matter – someone is able to change. Together you create a new space to grow.

You are right. This is why you came here today, not to write tomorrow's lecture. Do you see how it is? When your intent is clear/ vibrant the right time/place? So it is with being here on earth. The same. Clear/vibrant intent has brought you to the right place/earth at the right time/now to issue in the new era. For truly it is a new era as the old passes away, as you step into your lightbody* and teach others. By example, by words, by sharing. It is all one. So be it. We love you. Unconditional.

And I love you. Unconditional.

All is well.
Abide. Faith. Hope. Charity. All one.

Thank you.

*As our vibrational frequency increases, we become less dense in the physical.

September 18-19, 1998

Good morning, Shilogh. (I see him at the forest edge. Seems he's come to give me a pep talk for this program at the library. He stamps his feet, puts his arms and head up and down.)

Good morning, loved one, beloved. Early peace. You are up and about my business. It is good. You bring/give my message to the world. It is good. Be not afraid/fear not that you step too far into the spiritual. People are ready for the spiritual. People want to be invited. Yes. Invite them. They enjoy more themselves, being invited. Apologize not for how you do things. Merely bring to their attentions how *you* do things.

They will choose to follow or not. But you be the leader. You are the leader, making clear a path for them. Shine in what you do. You are worthy of shining.

It is worthy. They are worthy. Carry forward the torch of your shining.

Break open your self that they see light which is you. Those who are ready, see it. Others want to – so that is a beginning for them.

Press not, but allow. Always allow. " Let," yes, is a good word you use in the lecture. "Let" or allow.

Thank you. "Allow" is a good word, also.

Allow and be bright. Your lovingness shines from you. Others bask in it and respond. Be gentle as you are. Be easy. All is well. All is light.

Intrepid. Understanding. Full of itself. So be it.

Thank you. I honor you. I appreciate you. As the sun comes up, I remember you. Namaste.

Abide. (I hear or remember, Abide in me. I am the way and the light.) Yes.

Yes. Amen. Thank you. Adieu.

Je vous en prie.
Sleep now, a little more, dear one, and awake refreshed, rested, full of joy. You are so special.

September 20, 1998

Thank you for the successful conference yesterday. (I'm invited back next year.)

We are good together.
Yes. high on table.
Yes. high in tree.
Yes. high on mountaintop.
(Sun breaks through and touches my face.)

September 26, 1998 Chair. Meditating.

Be wary of trapping yourself in circumstances you don't approve. Take your own time. Impose your own structure, answers. Be not hasty, then. Be aware. Test against new that you're learning. Yes. Enough for now. *You* take charge and co-ordinate to your needs. We urge you.

October 2, 1998

Thank you for the help I will give today. (Sharon teaches this phrase.)

You're welcome. We love you. You are blessed. Thank *you* for carrying our message of good will to those you touch with your words and with your presence. All is well and does continue forward. As you go, does spread outward from you light and hope and freedom.

Think not that lazy reactions of students are the real message back to you. Students conceal what it is they really get from you – for fear it isn't real or may not last – by showing disinterest in the words. Which is correct response as what they get/receive is the message encoded in the words. You notice how they light individually with your attention. You see this. Be not surprised they would like this always instead of group. Days are made for this gifting. No gift is forgotten.

Thank you for the many evidences of love coming to me. I appreciate them and they make me smile.

You are welcome. It is our pleasure to see you smile. The tai chi book is a good idea. We like that. We'll help. Yes, symbol for Serenity is a good cover. In brush strokes.

Yes. Be willing to share stories and tips for journal to gather energy. This project you are not doing alone. You may do with others who are eager to help you. Flattered to help you. Oh, boy. We like this project. We see ourselves in it. It is time. You are right. It is time.

*(Right here typing this from notes onto the computer, everything froze and I couldn't do anything, even get out. So I shut down everything. Then I remembered, because of an approaching thunderstorm, I had

asked, *Please let me know when it's time to shut down.* "It is time" is the last thing I typed and couldn't even save. *Thank you.* I love it.)

You know, I'm concerned that important things happen and I don't remember them. I remember a bird hit the window here – at writing room – after an important insight. But I don't remember the insight. Please help me with this so I remember.

It is there. All there and you access it as you need it/can use it so you're not always balancing it with new stuff. It doesn't cost you energy. Yes. We'll help access as needed/useful. Have already begun.

Yes. Thank you.

Shall we write?

Yes. Let's.

All is well. So be it. Amen.

Thank you. Namaste.

You say Namaste; we bow.

October 6, 1998

> At tai chi last night, Ed said, "I see the landscape in your eyes. Every time I look at them. My grandmother would tell me, 'Look in the eyes. That's how you tell a person is living his life.' The landscape isn't one I've seen," he says. "Looks like it could be the southwest. Very old, very wise ones will have the landscape in their eyes."

October 6-7, 1998 dreaming asleep

> I see a round pine cone full of green light. It comes into my body. First in my chest, seems, under my right shoulder. Then I see it again in front of me. Pull it into my heart where it radiates good health, good energy.

Thank you for my pine cone. (Hear a pop somewhere in the room.)
Thank you for touching me so I know you are near.
Thank you for holding me so I know I am loved.
Thank you for noises around me.

October 10, 1998

Someone wants to know about anger.

I'll talk to you of anger.

Anger is a warning which tells you you are not a vibrational match for the situation you find yourself in. It is separation when there is no separation. It is a feeling of powerlessness, an act of giving power away. Let anger inform you. When you use anger at others to identify the place you feel separation from yourself, you guide yourself toward healing the separation.

If you are angry at someone else for acting inconsiderate, use it as an indicator. Look within, asking, Where in my life am I inconsiderate?

Recognize "being inconsiderate" as part of who you are – not separate from you but a possibility within you.

You will find that when you recognize and honor it, the cause of *that* anger can stop manifesting in your outer circumstances.

Don't separate the you that is angry. That shadow self is necessary for the *energy* of creation. We go through the shadow to integrate it with the positive to generate creative energy. Don't try to get rid of it. Circle it with love and use it.

Appreciation gets you off it pretty fast. That is, finding something you can send your energy toward will raise your vibration to a better match.

Use the contrast to help you decide what you *do* want and get on to that.

October 14, 1998

You are on the right path/way. Things will now go smoothly. Be not impatient. More energy is coming, more activity. You're going to love it as you actualize your dreams. There is stardust around you now. Soon there will be stars. As each piece comes together with other pieces, rejoice. Celebrate our love. As we celebrate you.

Dance.

As you begin to merge with the light, feel the twinkles at your outer edges; let yours expand.

October 14-15, 1998 dreaming asleep

> I've said I'll check Gram's every day while she's away. I go up the front stairs. As I come to the top, I see the banister, think here's where I feel something. Oh, it may not be resistance as I'd thought. It may be an angel. I've reached the porch, look in the window as I think that, holding a paper fan up to the glass so I can see in. See neat doors for cupboards/closets and the dear space of Gram's dining room. As I say, "Maybe it's an angel," I hold up the fan so Gram can see the reflection of an angel if one's there. I feel a large gust of wind push me against the house. Yup. It's an angel, I confirm. Wake.
> (Gust of wind is telling me what I just thought is correct. Awake and writing this, the thought comes to me, what she'll see is me – I'm the angel. To her, the angel she sees is me.)
> *Gram, I love you. I love your house* (even looking in the window gives me the feeling of love with her).

October 17-18, 1998

(Shilogh wishes to speak. He stands at the edge of the forest, a little to the left. Long trailings of beautiful feathers from his bonnet. He looks off to the left, not at me, as if he is thinking, raises one eyebrow.)

Shilogh, yes.

You are doing well. Don't you find it easy? Of course. The path is being cleared for you to follow/step into your dreams . Don't be stingy (as I reach for more of the papers I keep to write on at night and get 2). Don't be greedy (as I grab a bunch).

Everything in right amounts. Right amount of work and enjoying work's rewards. Right amount of having play. Important. You're right. The project becomes play/fun/reward when answers come every time – instead of only when you're working/focussing on them. When they come as gifts while you're walking or in the tub.

Why does it take me so long to figure out what I could be doing to be on my path?

Everything is training for everything else. Even this – that you see now – is the path only of this moment. Then the path goes on to the next moment and event.

You are right when you see that all you have done has been getting ready for this. And this gets you ready and on and on. Isn't it wonderful? Exciting? For me it is. And for you, too. We are quite good for each other.

How am I good for you?

In having to/choosing to steer you, I have quite a challenge. You listen so much to yourself. I first have to get your attention. Spend creativity to do this. Dress like this so you notice. Be creative and hold the frame to be credible. Or I lose you off to something else. You are good for me for my reward. When it works – what I do – you listen. I feel good. It is not mine to make you go certain ways but only to show you ways. When you're not looking with me, this I cannot do. So now, when you see me, I am complete in what I am with you. Feels good. Same way you feel good when you greet me and we speak. I rejoice as well. Celebrate like that.

Your prayer, "*Thank you for the help I will give today,*" invites me to you. Invites others, also. Invites the good you can be and the good that can help you. Why? Because what you are saying is, let me be used for good – for helping. This is good. And why you find (pop noise) situations in every day where you can help. Are you happy (having fun)?

Yes.

Uncle Leo says hi. He likes the lawn/yard there where you cleaned up. Agrees with John, don't lift things too heavy. Call on John to do them. He will, you'll see. You *are* making heaven on earth and this is appreciated. You'll see. You'll see. (They all applaud, surrounded in light as of a cozy bright place.)

You are invited.

We'll come. Watch for us and you'll see. Yes. Get up now. We'll come again. (Shilogh stands to the side watching this as if he is the narrator/MC, the guide. And he is.) I love you, (he closes, prayer hands and bows. I do, also.)

And thanks.

Adieu.

CHAPTER FIVE

Teachers, you are. Bringers of the light.

October 20, 1998 morning as I drive to school

A meditation:

Know yourself that you not be clouded over by the thoughts/the acts of others.
Know yourself well that your light may shine clearly.
Trip not your own self with "I wants" and wishes for what cannot be.
But do instead what is yours to do. Be what is yours to be. For in the long day, all is well – though it is the short span which commands your focus.
In the long day your responsibility is your own path, not the correction of others. As you change yourself, all else must change. Be not surprised at this.
If you would have people come to you, be comely.
For as you are at peace, they are invited.
As you are distressed, they hold back.
Temper your outrage with love to invoke clarity.
Each one has a purpose. Be assured.
All is well. Much love is here for you and you and you.

October 21-22, 1998 evening

Talk to me of peace.

Let's talk of peace. Peace is cultivated in the heart, nurtured, protected, encouraged. But peace does not stay there. No. It spreads, reaching to the hearts of others, creating a soft, a filmy…

(I sleep and wake)

Peace forms a web, a soft mist, a cluster of stars, whatever you would call it. The name is not important so that you understand it as energy which links between the heart and other hearts.

Whatever image gives you the impression that this is real, tangible, felt, not imagined. It is hard to make it clear, the luminous fibers we see connecting hearts. Difficult to describe in terms of the five senses. But know it is there.

Across distance and time Love is always. And peace comes from knowing that. As love resides, peace emerges. Take not onto your self the peace of the world as a foreign concept. For truly, the peace of the world is in you. The peace of the world is not something you must make in the world or ask to be brought to the world.

Peace *is*. In the world as it is in you. You do not understand this fully as you keep looking for external events and saying, But…

No but. When peace is in you – as you recognize and appreciate the love and so radiates from you only love – so needs be peace in the world. It cannot be other. It cannot be – waiting for someone else to do something – to talk peace talks.

See in your heart Love is always.

Hear in your heart Love is always.

Taste in your heart Love is always.

Smell in your heart Love is always.

Touch in your heart Love is always. And it is so.

From the love you are comes peace. It is simple. Be not influenced. Be simple. Be in touch. All is well. You are greatly greatly loved. Be at peace.

Amen. Adieu.

Good friends.

October 27, 1998

I'm doing the qigong (a healing form of Tai Chi) centering set, see, out the window, the tree, the grass with leaves in it, the sky, and certain soft motion which, as I watch, becomes pale hands, unnoticeable, almost, except I am seeing with soft eyes, my hands reflected on the window glass. I hear "These are the hands of god on this planet."

The tree, the grass, the sky, the hands
Blossoming
Give to the universe
Take back from the universe
And certain soft knowing these are the hands of god on this planet.

November 11-12, 1998

(Shilogh comes and puts his hand stroking my head.)

Be at peace, little one. Be easy. All is well. A flurry now, yes, but bringing you to new level/new heights. Enjoy. All is well. You are greatly loved.

Yes, important, as you said, that people talk about angels or whatever-you-call-them. Because the veil is thinning, truly thinning. This is because we wish it and you wish it, too.

It is a dream that you dream every step of. How it will be. It is changeable, changing. Be wary of forgetting it's a dream you create. It hasn't substance though it has impact. You allow the impact and so you learn. There is nothing you *must* learn; only that you will learn.

You would do well to be at peace, for later when you see what cause you have for peace, you will see no cause to be frantic.

Productive is good, yes, in a soft way, gentle way. It will be accomplished. All is well. Get up and go and be productive and revel in it.
We celebrate.
Adieu.

November 13-14, 1998
Mary-Shilogh to me

Yes. We have a message. You are greatly loved. You are all greatly loved. Do not take it for granted, this love, as if it is a small thing. It is a large thing. Powerful. That our light shines from this kingdom down to you. And through you to the world. Don't take it lightly. Oh, that. Don't fear to accept it. It is for you. Even as it is for you to share with others, it is for you to enjoy. It is no small thing, your coming together, your finding what you seek, your accepting of others' wisdom (goosebumps). It is exciting/a wonder/marvelous of you. Rejoice. The time *is* quite fast now. Haven't we told you? Enjoy now and now and now because when it comes, it is very fast. But the energy that comes with it makes it right/stable, as it should be/completes itself to be.

Now rejoice in each other that you know yourselves consciously. Congratulate yourselves for the trust you have placed in your own knowing of your purpose. You have confirmation of what you have known. And now you know it together. Happy day. We are complete in the first parts. Go with the urgency. But don't be swept away. Everything in its time. Your willingness is all. What could have been accomplished separately (and was/is) now is amplified among you. Let it be known. It is right and fitting that each now know your group.

Teachers, you are. Bringers of the light, that is love, that is Us. Isn't this how we started? Here we are again, but knowing it. Yes, Randeane. Your dream of a space ship bringing love. Yes. You have clarity in your dreams and in this new context will understand them more. Know it from the inside out. Love. Not just from hearing it or how it should be. But knowing it as *is*, as you are coming to do. When you accept that you are loved as well as loving, you allow someone near you/next to you, to accept this also. And so it is important, many times important. Not just *for* you but *through* you. Do you see? Yes. You know this. Do you use it?

Much love. Adieu. Fare thee well. Abide.

November 14-15, 1998
(Shilogh dressed in leggings with fringe that moves as he stamps his feet in moccasins.)

We are making power. Making thunder. Making rain for seeds to grow. You'll see. The seeds you have planted. You are meant to teach the universe* and so we will help by making power. Watch for it to come. Watch for how to use it. All is ready. Are you?

I think so.

Keep thinking so for here it comes. The great rain. Weather through, knowing what it is for, how to use it. As it comes to you. Direct it in ways you are knowing. This magic trick is useful. Linking two hands so each knows what the other is doing (this refers to muscle checking which I've just learned). Like taking a vote with the right of you, the left of you, no? All in harmony, go ahead. All not sturdy, please wait. Hand signals, no? Like smoke signals. Know how to read them. All is ready now. Stand ready, too. Soft eyes. Alert. Being calm and being watchful and acting on time, when locked fingers give you a signal.

We like the party Monday. We are amused. In a good way, only. Delighted. Thank you for your honors. We receive. (Bows head to me with right hand on heart – sign language?) Yes. Means we respect you and accept how you honor us because for you we have greatest respect. It is so.

You will please join us, then?

We are there, already. Eating cookies. (He laughs, shows me with two hands, he's eating cookies. Others are around in groups in costume though obviously see-through angels. They are in the office. And we haven't come to start yet.)

*At qigong class some months ago, the teacher asked us to get quiet, picture a computer screen, and ask the universe for a message. My message came immediately, "You are meant to teach the world."

November 15-16, 1998
For someone

Writing is really messages to ourselves and others. It's slowing for a moment our innermost thoughts to see them and give them form. We write to celebrate who we are. And to learn who we are. And to remember who we are. And we are powerful beings. We write to claim our power. To recognize it and to claim it. For as we put the pen onto paper or allow letters onto the screen, we give permission to ourselves to inform us and make us whole.

We speak of angels and higher self. We speak of spirit guides and totems. However we choose to name our connection with the godself, with the I Am, with the all that is, writing is ours to let it, to reach it, to touch it, to allow it to teach. So that we hear what it speaks in a mode we can go back to and see again and assure ourselves is real. In a form that is enduring. So we can read it again, assure ourselves again that we didn't make that up. As we let our spirit inform us, we learn what spirit is. And walk the path of spirit, hearing what it says.

November 19-20, 1998

These messages you send arrive safely. You are known. You are known for your loving unconditional love. All is well. All is well. Good night.

Thank you.

Sleep well. Good night. (They are laughing because of how actively I sleep.)

November 21-22, 1998
For someone

I'm meaning to say I love you. This is a lot for you. Pick you up into my lap and hold you, rock you, soothe you. Tell you this *is* a safe place though it doesn't always seem it. Let you cry if you want and nestle and hold on tight to me if you want and let go. Howl and rage and I'll hold a safe space for you to do it until you've done all you want and can fall asleep in peace. Or dance. Swirling the beautiful star essence of you as you turn and leap and laugh into your joyous self. So that when you come to rest in twinkles of knowing, you know that All is well. All is truly well.

November 23-24, 1998 ~ dreaming awake

Shilogh?

Yes. We want to talk to you. This is not good, this giving yourself a headache so you can take the evening off. Stop it. You deserve an evening of rest when you know you need it. You have been working hard. You are working – that is using energy – hard, assimilating new information, new knowledge, new knowing.

As it is with you, it is with many. It is common not to take the time you need to slow and allow yourself to absorb what you need. Do it now. Pace yourself now. It is good that you recognize what you need. Didn't your students recognize also?

But don't hurt yourself, suffer yourself guilty over claiming what is yours, and taking what you need. Time is yours, yes, you see. To use as you choose for your highest good. This serves the good of others. You know this for other people, why keep it from yourself?

Take care of the foods you eat. You are getting sloppy. You do feel better without the sugars.

We bring you joy and good tidings. Yes. It is as you have been told my Patricia Nelson.* Haven't we told you? Yes. And your books will find their homes. The time is coming for this planet that the stories be seen as stories of light. And loved. And the new book will bring them to it. Those who were not yet ready when the stories were written are ready for them now. It is good and timely that they are in place. Now will they be recognized and hailed. Keep in close contact with Bronson Alcott who is here to help you, but don't let his serious side bind you over.

Remember to laugh and he will laugh, too. And that will be delightful. We are joyous for you. (I see them all in a group along the sidelines.) Be loved. You are so loved. You did the "right" thing to come home yesterday but it was not necessary to suffer. Love yourself as well as you did without suffering over it. We have scolded enough. You know we love you.

And I love you.

Yes. Adieu. Fare thee well. Abide.

*Patricia Nelson, in her afternoon workshop, Meet Your Guides, has told me Bronson Alcott is around me to help with the writing of books.

November 24-25, 1998

Let's see if there is anything.

You are loved, dear. Sweetly loved. This is so.

I do adore the gift and that you thought of it and wrapped it. Thank you.

(This from my guide, Mary Ann. I bought her lavender powder.)

November 30, 1998 afternoon meditation

Was wondering whether to go gift shopping

Stay. Focussed. Stay intent. As you intend, you draw what you are needing to you. We are here to help with this. Don't scatter energy we all could be using. Other things will wait and be complete at appropriate times.

An activity:

Decide what a gift "for me" would be. What is the gift? Is it received? How is it received? How does it come to you? If it hasn't yet come, be open to receiving. Practice noticing what comes to you and whether what comes might fit what you asked for. Set up situations in which you give yourself gifts. Time, ease.

Be aware. Write out what happens next. Notice how closely the universe responds, often in a way unfamiliar.

December 2, 1998 morning meditation

(Have you been in touch with your son since he's living in the spirit world? I see myself asking someone and hear this about his son.)

He's all right. Living in the spirit world. He looks like you.

He's saying, "Dad, fall in love with yourself. *You* are worthy."

He loves you. He doesn't see why you don't. All is forgiven, he says, where he is, all is forgiven and loved without measure. He's been trying to get in touch. He's happy that he's reached me.

This is a message I give to your dad? Yes.

Is this from his son? Yes.

(Delicious waves of goosebumps.)

Is your name Dan? No. Gabriel. His name there is Gabriel.

Thank you, Gabriel.

(Extreme goosebumps.)

December 5-6, 1998 dreaming asleep

> "We came because you promised peace," someone I meet along a wall at some ancient town tells me.

December 8, 1998 morning
For someone

You are important to my plan. It's why you have spent such time evading it. You have the sense of wanting control. Be in control as much as you want, and when you release, come to me. Come to me in whatever guise is comfortable, from whatever need you must, or from curiosity. It matters not.

You can help in our purpose here on earth. You can enlighten from being enlightened. You can speak your story with authority to those who need to listen. Think not that any of you was in vain. For all of it is important.

As you make yourself different characters, different characters will find you. Doubt not that out of your feelings – intense and frantic feelings – comes your love, comes your light. And those who would see you, will see you and know that you speak truth.

It is not preaching that I say here, but setting by example. All that you may choose to do is setting an example for those of the earth who will follow. Take not lightly your abilities in this regard.

People are made of stuff like you. And people will learn from you. Make clear with yourself what your message will be and learn it well for others.

For as you clear your message, your light does clear and many there are who will see it and know peace.

All is well. So be it. Adieu.

December 11-12, 1998

(The one who was in the hospital has now gone on and I sense her in the spirit world.)

I hope that message I gave you in the hospital was all right, I say to her now.

It was what I needed.

Thank you. I knew it, but I needed to hear it. It was a brave thing, dear.

It was how you connect with self and truest self. That was the also importance of that message.

Thank you. Are you comfortable?

I am in light. I am learning as I wish.

I think I saw you at Reiki at your house.

Yes. With my circle of friends. That was to connect my husband with Reiki also. What I went through. You know that. So now he has Reiki to give. He is a healer who now has a tool, an instrument for healing. He does not know yet his power in this world. In the circle around him. He can cause such good. Does cause such good.

Is it okay to tell him this?

Of course.

And about the message?

The message is for me.

Yes. That's as I thought.

He can know about it, but that was not its purpose. It is for me and, in the way I said, for you.

Yes. Thank you.

All is well.

Truly well. Thank you.

December 12, 1998 a meditation circle

> Sitting in the meditation circle, I see Shilogh's face for the first time. Edna Adamson sits across from me and after the circle, says, "You feel palpitation here (at the heart) because they're close. You feel someone very close behind you, but turn to look and don't see anyone. Someone is very close. And writing. Don't put it off. You want to do it, but get busy doing something else. They want to write with you. From this you can even get a book."

December 12-13, 1998

Shilogh

Thank you for coming.

You are welcome. I let you see my face because you are ready to see my face. You have come a long way to see it, and don't forget me.

Are you the man on the horse I saw in a dream a couple of years ago?

Am I? Yes I am. I will come sometime and take you on my horse.

I will like that.

Will you? We'll see. It is a learning journey. Be ready.
The woods are beautiful now and we can smell the wood smoke.
Simplify. If not having all the time to write, simplify.
Christmas, as you have thought. The gifts to charity.
Sit in the quiet. Don't skip that. Usually you don't skip it. Sit it like sitting a horse, alert and aware to where it might take you.
Christmas will come and be past. Just allow it to go.
The book is very important. More important than you know.

I value your words, brother.

And we, here, value yours. (He sits now on the horse where I am wont to see him at the edge of the woods. He speaks of the woods now. But his chest is bare.)

We watch. We help. Be silent and let us. Listen.

December 14, 1998 in meditation

Good morning, Shilogh. (I see him.)

Good morning. We would speak. (I think he means we – he and horse.) Yes. My horse and I would speak you greetings. All is well.

Who was the other voice? (something for me before this)

One of the brethren/sistren (taps) keepers of the world and peace. But not one in the sense that you speak one, meaning, separate. One in the sense that we speak one, meaning, all of us. And so I am in that voice as well. But/And come to you like this, familiar. Comfortable, no?

Yes.

Cozy, in your words. *Yes.* (For my highest good? I muscle check and the answer is, Yes.)

Thank you for checking (He's smiling. Amused.) so I know I am what I (sparkle of taps) think I am/so I know I am for your highest good. (He takes my hand and swings it in his.) Now we can relax and enjoy this company. Now we can get on ahead in no time with no hesitation. Yes?

Yes.

The writing is going apace. Whatever interrupts is fine. Be not disturbed. It rights itself. Its balance is assured. Yes.

Your guides are very happy in writing. Even now, that the pen is in the hand. It all counts. All the words. All the blessings. We do our work together and make it play, make it sing, make it dance. No wonder people love you – like doing dishes at the church, yes, that feel of many hands and many hearts making play of the earth work.

It is so as well in my kingdom (tap). But here we make even lighter. (He holds something – a ball or bowl that on earth would have weight (tap) and shows how light it is where he is – really no weight at all. He is amused and playing with this, delights to show me.)

Please let us help you keep the lightness of this bowl. (I see it now radiating (tap) light and he is smiling, See?)

The work on the writing continues. Time will be there for that. Relax and let us guide you. Relax and be at ease.

All will be well with the writing. All is being well right now. Did you not receive the congratulatory roses from our angel Michael and know it is complete? (Roses from Michael delivered in dream the other night – completion, grounding, manifestation on the earth plane.)

Are you feeling centered now? Grounded and complete?

Much better, thank you.

You are busy, yes. And happy in being busy. Take time also (tap) for yourself – and for us, as well.

Thank you. You are welcome here.

We feel it. Amen. (He puts his hand up, stands with his horse.)

What part of the message did the horse bring?

All of it. (He laughs.) Without him, I am not very bright. (He shows himself dim and smaller. Then laughing, his own bright self. The horse is laughing also.)

Thank you, both.

I check, is this really happening? Yes. Then see a whole audience there, semi-circle laughing and applauding. I think, I guess in the show I'm the fool. Shilogh stops laughing and becomes stern and takes up the whole picture.

What are we telling you? You are important, necessary. Not the fool, no. But able to take yourself lightly. (Now the twinkle is back. He bows Namaste.)

Namaste. And thank you for coming.

Ah, but *you* are *our* guest. And thank you. (taps)

Adieu. Fare thee well.

December 14-15, 1998 asleep dreaming

> "An extension of Christ consciousness…that is being enlarged.
> And it's being done through molecules." I was seeing light,
> almost a hole of light – formed by light around the edges. Seems
> extending into space/infinity – all light – no darkness (noise of
> shifting, something shifting above me). At the same time seeing
> the light from a tiny Christmas bulb – how it radiates. Light
> like this expanding – molecules.

December 17-18, 1998 awake

Look into yourself. See you are complete and whole and ready to
enter your higher level of being.

Open your eyes. And see one other person. And see that you are
loved. And show that person he is loved.

You keep yourself in darkness. No one else can. Open your eyes and
see the light around another person. And unlimit your beliefs. With
love in your heart, project light to the other person and accept love for
yourself. Help each other hold the energy that you are loved. Check
within that this is true. Let limitation fall from you. And turn your self
to others and include them in your love. And hold safe space for those
who are struggling to remember they are divine.

Honor your godself and the godself of others. Don't follow others'
gods. Honor your own godself. See if you are ready to walk in light with
lighter body and greater love.

No keys will bring you what you already have within.

We invoke Source, whatever that is for you. We remember that we
are divine energy expressing god on this planet. We remember how to
do that in love. We remember peace begins in the heart with good intent.

The keys to what you seek are within you. Find them. Let there be
peace on earth and let it begin with me.

December 19-20, 1998 (Refers to Edna at meditation circle last week.)

Shilogh?

Edna is right. When you feel the flutter in your throat, it is your spirits near and wanting to use your voice.

Yes. You sometimes put 2 and 2 metaphor together and you sometimes don't, so I will tell you. Maybe it is me. I like the "Ho." It shows respect. It also uses forceful breath to project the word into being. Try this "Ho." Play with it. See for yourself.

It is so exciting to work with someone who understands this, or when she doesn't understand, says, "I will try this." Because then things can happen. It is why and because your chakras are balanced that this be so. Your child (Katherine)* uses these words wisely. "Why because." She understands the deep meaning of them.

Let us talk about prayer and how you have been praying. Prayer is an attitude more than words. Words are the ritual form, the shaping. The words are lovely beings that carry your intent. Think of them with wings, yes, flying . . . but where? Upward you see them. But what is upward? Where do they go? Yes. They go into other hearts. The way this child's (Katherine's) words reach you and you know them, prayer words reach other hearts – on this world and beyond, the hearts of those appropriate to the words and, yes, the word vibrations reach what we name Source, but all along the way – as you would see it – they touch the hearts of others. Be wary, or aware. Your thoughts speak and your actions speak. And they are heard. As your thoughts and actions vibrate the same as your words, so are your prayers then heard. This is how it is. Let your every action and being be in vibration with your words that hearts may hear clear message and respond with clear purpose. So it is with prayer.

All is well. You are healing your knee now that you know about it. And we are helping now that we know your intent. All is well. You are greatly loved. Ho!

Ho.

Ho. Merry Christmas.

Thank you and you, too.

Adieu. Fare thee well. Abide.

*Katherine the Great is the fictional reality at our house.

December 20-21, 1998
For someone

Okay. We see it that he sees you can make it on your own, fine without him. School, friends, social, success. Finding directions. Everything. You would do well to remind him that you didn't come to this place in your homey apartment to be in school, only. You came to be in school *and* be with him the way both of you yearned to be. Help him remember what dreams you dreamed then. Help him see how close you've come (to the dreams you set). It is not to forget those dreams now you have become them, but to honor and appreciate.

How can you hope to achieve the next dreams without recognizing you have achieved these ones and showing honor by appreciating.

This young man would do well to learn appreciation now. Spend minutes of time in gratitude. This would quiet him enough to notice. It may be that a home ritual would help him do this, a family practice he hasn't had before. You see it in him when he loves the cat sometimes. That automatic joy he can be in touch with when he forgets enough himself.

A ritual we mean of simple notice. A rock, a feather, something he notices for a few moments. On a daily basis. Words. "I appreciate…. I appreciate…." would put him in touch with his loving nature.

This can be done, but not by saying "We must do this." You may have to teach. You are a teacher. He hasn't been taught this. Be creative. Look at books on meditation. Native American chants. Celtic wisdom. Let him devise his heart's prayer of thankfulness. All will be well. This is an important meeting of you two. You are right not to hold on tightly. This little boy in a toy store still yearns to be taken home. Into love. Into being needed and important.

When you see him as needed and important as well as loved, this is your appreciation. Your appreciation creates the space for all good changes in this one. Forget not to begin, very begin with thankfulness in yourself. Maybe make a list in words if you both like lists. It is enough for now.

December 24-25, 1998 dreaming asleep

> I see a beautiful slender god or buddha statue of stone. In robes a (small circle) on its forehead. Meditation pose in lotus position with hands on knees, mudra position, finger and thumb together. Beautiful soft golden pink light.

Awake:

Buddha, do you wish to speak?

Appreciate me. (I'm to look at buddha, appreciate the beauty as I write the dreams.)

Anything else?

> You are loved. You are greatly loved. From the highest heavens you are seen and loved. Know that you are holy. Know this day is for you. To celebrate. Make merry. Give love. Receive love.

Adoration?

> Yes. Adoration. And these gifts that come to you. Receive them lightly and not lightly for they are truly given. Given with love. And it is yours to accept love however it comes. In accepting, you are giving. You see how this is so. (I was understanding, yes. My appreciation is a gift. Oh. Appreciate because appreciation is also a gift to the giver. Appreciate you as a gift to you.)
> You see clearly. All is well.

Thank you.

Adieu. Be well.

Thank you, beautiful buddha. (Star. There is a star. I see it in front of him, to the left, about the level of his forehead.)

The star is coming to you. Watch for it. And clarity.

What is this star?

Clarity. Coming to you in full abundance. Dance. Be merry and light-hearted with this. Not sober and sombre. Delight. It is a gift you have wanted because it is yours, belongs to you.

Has it to do with the third eye?

Yes. And much more. To do with all of you, and who you are and what you are doing here. You are courageous in wanting to know. In wanting to do what you came here to do. In wanting to carry your part. You are greatly admired. And appreciated. Thank you.

Watch for it. Everything will change. Yes. Watch for it means being open as you understand. (Being open as in finding the pin for Audrey when I wasn't looking for one. Open to all channels to receive.)

Yes. You have it. Good way to explain it.
(Muscle test. This message is from an Ascended Master? Yes.)
(Then, I'm remembering, angels in a circle around me in the night. Then, a woman to my left. Shiny old red truck in front of me. We get in and take off. Airborne.)

December 25-26, 1998 dreaming asleep

Oh, God invites me onto his knee and like Santa, says, "What would you like?"
Comfort and grace, I tell him without thinking. Now I think of all I could have asked for!

The other you have, he tells me. All that you can think up. And this you have as well but would like it to manifest strongly. It will. You don't even have to be patient. You are already patient and this is coming. It has to come.

(God is shaking his head that I would get down from his knee to write this, and now I'm afraid of not being welcome/invited back.) You are invited again and again, (He shakes his head with a twinkle) as often as you like.

He pushes his hands, fingertips down, in front of him as if to say, Scamper off. And I do. I feel like a faery child. Delighted. I come back to the world.

January 5-6, 1999 ~ dreaming awake

Writing is a tool/a path for your deepest wisdom/highest guidance. Writing is not something you push across the page like a snowplow but something you allow to draw you across the page, dancing. If you would write, don't push your meaning across the page, but allow it to draw you into places you didn't know were there.

Ah. Look. I didn't know that. Oh. See what he's gone and done. Be gentle with yourself. Be allowing. Be encouraging the way you would encourage others. Encourage yourself.

Jan 11-12, 1999 ~ dreaming awake

I'm singing symbols in my head. I hear, "Speak a protection."

Great Spirit, hear my words to the north and the south and the east and the west. Hear my words.
Protect us here as we go about your sacred work. Guide us here as we go about the work of spirit. Love us here as we honor you and love you and follow your word, that all be one. That all know love. That all know comfort and strength and the power of right-doing, sacred-doing, in attunement, alignment with One. (flutter throat feeling)
Be with us, we invite you with our songs of joy. Ho.

Many blessings, dear one, for you are dear to us. Querido, (dear one,) we would call you and you know our meaning. Good morning, Bright Star. Your mother named you well, for you are the Bright Star of your people. We have come to help you manifest, for your faith is great. Truly, your faith moves mountains (energy sparkles – I see these mountains = obstacles, doubt, clouded thinking) so clear light can shine in.

Truly you bring light. (I see light hitting what used to be in the shadow of the mountain.)

We are here to help you stand on your own. It will be lonely, but you won't be alone. And you are good at lonely. You have discovered it, ridden it, and come through.

Congratulations and plaudits. Applause. You are doing well. Follow your dreams. You are enlightened (I see sunlight on mountains and where mountains have been – sunlight) like sunlight on the mountains.

See how you shine around you onto others' mountains. Yes. And others (people at writing workshop).

Yes. And be you the sunshine on tomorrow's meeting of the minds. Be you the light and guidance. Set the tone for harmony so harmony can fill it. Set the tone for light so light may stream in. All is well.

Thank you.

Thank you, child of light.

January 11-12, 1999 dreaming asleep

"God is good at this peace and love. Lots of practice. He needs us to bring it to earth," I hear and wake.

Before this in the dream, someone tells us, "Every 13 feet or every 21 feet." I understand this in the dream. Means there's a love tie-down/ anchor every 13 or 21 feet.

Some people have fear, though. Even the drummers. I see the drummers with, or one drummer with, a sort of fog at his left side the length of his torso.

So we're needed to bring it here for those who might be fearful – or because there are still those who are fearful.

Jan 12-13, 1999 ~ dreaming awake

The child is fine. The snarl-ups are things she needs to learn, is ready to learn. This may give a new direction. Is she looking at all aspects of each situation? Ice/sand on the road? In her life situation? Or hoping to drive over them without spinning out – going down the incline – hurting someone else?

She is fine. And sturdy. She needs to listen to her feelings – her warnings – not cover them in sand to think she's safe. To think they're not there.

With (the young man) she needs to do this, too. To be aware. Watchful of the road. Aware to change speed or direction in response to what is needed. Give herself time to steer in control.

She is lucky, yes. She has had a warning to proceed with caution – not to scare her – but to wake her up to be aware.

To watch how (the young man) handles this and learn what can be learned.

All is well. She learns much by this about all kinds of things. Let her draw to her now the goodness and light that are hers. She is also a bright star who has much to give.

January 30-31, 1999

Good morning, Shilogh.

Have you forgotten me?

Um. Yes, I have.

No matter. You remember me when you need me.

Any help about these books?

They will find their own homes. We have told you. Not to worry. They are beautiful books. Glorious books. With wings. You are right to save them, protect them. They are like wild things needing your protection now that the woods are not dense. Care for them now and give them a home. And then you can let them go.

Thank you.

Chapter Six

Be in fellowship with peace.

Feb 5, 1999 at Sharon Massoth's meditation, Sharon's guide told me this:

"It is magnificent that you are and it is this magnificence of love and kindness that you want to embrace others with. There are opportunities that are going to be given to you that you need to act on. You are the primary spokesperson for those who are authors and channels. You need to move into a place of acceptance of your knowledge of how you channel. Draw to you other authors who are channels. Be about publishing your own book of channeled guidance. Take your rightful place. Open to guidance is for the whole world to receive. Touching people is your wish. You will be touching many people who would not be reached because they are accessible only by books and written form.

"You will bring **HOPE** to scores of people that their lives are valuable and they are valuable.

"Blessings!"

I ask about this and receive these answers from Sharon's guide:

Am I to act as a channel and write what I receive?

"Yes. Ready to actually be a channel – channel a book to be received by many. You have the credentials and the authority. Educating others on the reality of channeling."

Just be open in channeling? or helping other writers to their knowing – writing channeled guidance?

"You think too much. When you are with yourself, you will have the answer. Divine self – not head will give you the connection with helping beings – you will know what to write. Go to the sacred place you know. Ask. Connect. Let it happen.

"You already have the connection. When you are thinking of guides, it's easier for them to reach you. You become a more conducive channel. An incredible inspirational force."

I'm to channel a book and make it clear that it's channelled.

"This is different than the stories. You may still be writing the stories. By inspiration. But also be a pure channel and write the channeled book. It's in your heart. Your head just doesn't know it. Get to the sacred place. Say, 'Let's commence the book,' and listen to your heart. Your heart knows."

(I ask on the way home:)

What is it you want the world to know?

It's time for love in greater abundance than ever before.

Let's commence the book.

Feb 6, 1999 dreaming asleep

"You are the philosopher's stone." Transmitting energy into manifestation. (I think this means channeled book into published words – their message into the world) and it does.

Feb 6-7, 1999 falling asleep

Let me talk to you of love/sorrow. Love which encompasses grief. Love which is aching to treasure each part of existence for itself and for its teachings. Nothing is without the truth it brings. Nor can they be separated. The experience from its truth. Love seeks, then, to feel into every crack and deepest part, whatever truth experience brings.

Give us, then, this sorrow. That we may turn it to the light. Give us then, this heaviness which seems to hide, turning self away from itself. This cannot be. Nor can it separate from its truth. But in the trying, causes pain, causes that which is unhappy, unglad, yes, unjoyous.

Rather, let love embrace it. Rather let it turn itself toward light, that in turning what would hide from itself be seen. Be seen, stand tall, This, too, is what I am.

Let sorrow revel in sorrow, rejoice in itself, that not being hidden, it is free to choice. What would I say? Embrace it. Encircle it with love.

Let this be daily practice. Encircle it with love. For when sorrow is loved, it has dignity and need not cause you hurt. Yes.
(I'm asking what to call the bringers of this message.)

The Great Ones. You may call us the Great Ones. Sun Bear, you may call us. Angels. Wisdom, you may call us. Dreams. Fiery. Night Fathom. What you call us doesn't matter. *That* you call us does.

We are beloved of you. Call us. Please do. It makes us feel quite loved. Charmed/charming.

February 7-8, 1999

We would speak to you of sorrow. We would speak to you of greed. Greed is a hunger, a living force that compels you to want. But what it is you want cannot fill your need to have it. This is because what you want is communion with your spirit self from which you are estranged. Comfort with your spirit self which is you. Not separate, not different. You. You want something because you are hungry, yet it doesn't fill you up. You want something because you see it and it will make you happy, yet it does not make you happy. It is natural and appropriate that you want for yourself comfort. Yet the comfort you give to your little self does not serve the greater self that you are unless there is a recognition, an awareness in your being that you are whole. When, in your being, there is this recognition, then every act of comfort serves you. Only when you become aware that everything you need, you have, does the comfort of your little self serve your greater good.

Think not, then, to chase after this thing and that thing, but find in your self all the things of your wanting and then you will find comes to you that which comforts, brings you joy, and satisfies your love.

Appreciate from your place of want that place of spiritual longing. Appreciate and that place will be filled with sacredness. Watch this happen. Honor it for it is so.

February 7-8, 1999

Anger. Trust your anger to show you home. What is anger but expression of how lost from home you are? How untrusting of finding your way back.

But you have never left. You are not far from home. You are in home. Trust your anger to show you you don't know this. Let your anger lead you here. There is no place you're trying to get. There is nothing you're trying to be. Your anger leads you straightway into knowing this. Trust your anger to tell you.

Anger is your guidepost. Use it and go past. It directs and you follow. You don't have to hold onto the guidepost, once it has shown you your truth. Ultimately, anger is useful. Rebel not against the guide.

Anger and pride and righteousness get sometimes stuck together and hold each other up, you'll see. And prove each other right. Awareness releases them neatly. Awareness lets them go.

What can you do to resolve them? Make much of them, first, for making clear what they came to show you. Honor them. Appreciate. And then direct your attention at what it is they're showing you.

When the misperception has been balanced, the anger fades away. It is completed. Shun circumstances that cover anger's message.

February 7-8, 1999

Express your knowing. Act on it. Treat it with respect. Express it in ways that have meaning for you. Not for other people. Others are persuaded by their own knowing, not by yours.

February 8-9, 1999

Let us talk to you of speed.

Speed?

The quickness you are going. It is not necessary to do everything you do with a quickness that does not allow you to see things along the way, does not allow you to notice the good time you are having.

Making a blur of everything with the speed you are going does not help certain moments stand out sweetly in your experience, in your notice, in your remembering.

Speed robs away the color and the tone and the savoring of your moments.

What is speed? It is getting from here to there, somewhere to somewhere else, where you are to where you're going, without allowing your enjoyment.

Make your promise be to enjoy, not to get there, and you will arrive in shining colors and vibrant energy. You will arrive enriched and enrich those around you. Watch how this can be. With tiny motion, you arrive. Seeing each star in between, you arrive. Not out of breath, you arrive. In your own calmness, you arrive.

Watch a hummingbird. And notice how all else waits.

You are not meant for speed, but for enjoyment.

All is well.

Adieu.

We like this book. It is a good book.

Clearly define your goal and then zigzag your way to it. Circle around. Miss it completely and come back. Arrange to live each moment so none will be missed and all will be loved. When you appreciate the beauty, the balance in the moment, you create beauty and balance. Aptitude for speed drops away. Aptitude for pleasure closens.

Fast speed, we are meaning. Away from fast speed, spring still comes, more joyously.

February 9-10, 1999

We would speak of work. Are you ready? Work takes you places you wouldn't go and gives you situations you wouldn't choose to be.

Work invites you in, makes you at home with situations you would avoid that are for your learning. Think what you would avoid and not learn if you could. It is responsible and responsive that so many people choose work. Some for themselves, some for others they are protecting and nurturing – as with a family. And how appropriate for each the work that is chosen. He/she is choosing.

Look around you. People are making acts of courage, putting themselves in tests of strength and will. Daily. Because of making the agreement, "I will do this." Strength and will. Endurance. Safe-keeping. Wonder. Endurance. Appreciation. Regard. Respect. All the opportunities to learn are given in what you term work. And look how you regard it. Do you regard it with joy/ with thanksgiving? Or with dread, pulling your feet behind you to get there? What is the engagement of your being in this work?

We would tell you – play. We would tell you, take lightly what you have come to learn. Not to pry around it as a rock too heavy to move. But to dance around it in joyful remembering of its good will. Not as an adversary that must be accomplished, subdued, overcome, but as a partner that may be danced, given/taken, disarmed.

Give not to work all the armaments you would fight against. But rather lay down the fighting tools and dance with it in lightness, enlightened from accoutrements that are not needed, called for.

Here is opportunity to play. Engage with Spirit work. Here is chance. To encounter the beloved. Here is place to find footing and hold it lightly. We would speak of work which draws you out of what you have decided and made pat, firm, into what you may discover, allow. Freedom. When you don't allow, you are making limits. And limits draw to you limits. Look into your spirit of work and see what limits you have placed there which now you struggle under, with/against. They are of your own making.

And limits will call limits until you dance them free. Play them loose. Allow them to let go.

Work reminds us, doesn't it, how limitless we are. How free we choose to be, how allowing we may become.

Work is the play of divine spirit, letting go, releasing limitations you have chosen to hold.

Come with us now to work as a place of thanksgiving and joy. A place to free the spirit and see it soar. A place to take appropriate action and receive blessings and nurture love.

Being in allowance calls this nature to you.

Being in allowance frees the will to dance.

How will it be when you let yourself see this and act as if it is so? How will it be to create harmony that you are wanting?

Thank you angels. Thank you spirit guides, spirit helpers, spirit letters-me-help-you. Oh, that's where we get the word letters.

Harmony resonates.

February 10-11, 1999

Let us talk to you about patience. We would make the point that, although patience is a virtue, it need not be indiscriminately applied. Patience works best when it is applied in appropriate measure.

Some things are needing their push of impatience to move off some stuck point, for instance. Some situations call out for action instead of, or combined with, patience. The virtue of patience is in using it in appropriate response.

Think not that every situation resolves through your having enough patience – meaning you use "enough" to mean "more". You are using patience at times instead of doing action and this would be no virtue in the cases where action is the appropriate response.

We would teach you, then, to notice how your patience serves you. And how it works against what you would achieve for your highest good. We would teach you to *use* patience first and with awareness.

February 11-12, 1999

Rejoice. Rejoice. Emmanuel will ransom captive Israel.

Awareness. Awareness. For what are you striving? For what are you suffering? When you are Joy Incarnate. A slowing, thickening of energy into form. Be re-aware, re-awakening, remembering of this. Joy is awareness.

Seek not to confine it, limit it, shape it, for as you do, so do you limit your Self. Awareness unbinds the struggle you invite by forgetting, not seeing you are Joy Incarnate.

Act with that knowing now. What else you create, you create from not knowing this.

What your spirit knows. We remind you. In the still moments be aware of its truth. Unbind yourself from suffering by knowing this. Unbind yourself from struggle by awareness this is true/truth. Dance in the awareness. *This* awareness.

Is that all/complete?

You are deeply loved. We love you. All is well.

Take courage that this book is launched. It is the right book – the one we are wanting. We like to come to you. We like your words with ours. Translation pure. Thank you. This is fun. Don't you think?

Yes. I do. I love it. (They are smiling. A group of beings who remind me of men in togas or robes. 5 or 6 or 7 standing in golden rosy light, barefoot. Smiling. Feeling good. Seems like golden rose rocky cliffs behind them.)

February 12, 1999 morning
For someone

We would speak of courage. We would set aside your perception and remind you courage comes from god, from the link you have together with god.

Why do you think you have situations which demand courage if not to put you into remembrance of your link with god.

I don't know how I did it, you might say. Something beyond me. Bigger than I am. I didn't think that I could do it.

You try so much alone. That is not necessary. Remember your association with god. Remember you are unseparate. Notice, when courage comes, the connection it makes with Source. Notice, then, this connection in all things.

Why would you not be connected, – unseparate – at all times? Choose to notice and you will see. Though you call on it mostly in times in need of courage, always it is there.

Only you, in your thinking, separate, and you are making this up. Until you appreciate this, you will keep drawing times that need courage, to point it out.

February 12-13, 1999

Let us talk of stress. What is it except putting yourself in places to be pulled two ways. It would be better seen as stretch. Stress is when you fight against it. Stretch is when you grow. Stress happens when you are rigid, defining boundaries, defending boundaries, rules, the way-it-is.

Stretch is a flexibility and wonder. A curiosity and allowing. Think of a time that you call stress and you will see the resistance. You will see the holding on you do of something.

There is great truth here. It is not the situation that causes you stress, but the holding on. The trying to maintain some idea, some form, some structure you perceive.

We say let it go. We say allow the rigid pattern to stretch. There is no boundary between you and god. You can stretch all the way home to god.

The stress is a signal that you're not allowing this. Smile. And release the box you've placed around yourself. Recognize stress for what it is. The signal of a limitation. Smile, oh, yes. I see. I remember. And let the edges of the box subside. And stretch yourself. As you touch the godself to awaken, as you give the godself notice, the signal is no longer needed.

Be aware of stress in your life. Look for it. Honor it for showing you where you have made a limitation. Release the limitation. Let it soften and be flexible. So you may grow in to places you are wanting.

What is stress? Your own stretch when you hold against it. Be thankful for what it shows you. Keep it if that's what you choose. It will keep signalling. That is its job. That is its use. Or use it to see where to change. That is its value. Be aware. Abundance is letting go limitation. Allowing. Abundance all the way home.

Loneliness is separation. And there is none. Loneliness shows you are looking in a wrong direction. Be not lonely. Be embraced. With your own knowing who you are.

February 13-14, 1999

Laughter warms your heart and spirit. Be friends with laughter. Arrange your time, your day, to enjoy its company. Laughter comes as appreciation of the lightness of things. An appreciation of the joy in each moment. Let laughter ripple through you and burst though any blocks you are starting in your energy field. Laughter is a way to stay supple, and balanced, and flexible, and light. Laughter adds gracefulness to your being. Let laughter ripple through your etheric/energy/physical body and keep you light.

Wash your knees with laughter. Wash your feet that you find it easy to walk and take nourishment from mother earth. Wash your body in laughter that your organs stay refreshed. And wash your head in laughter that your dreams stay clear and bright.

Laughter is a friend to sit with and let go. We would tell you laughter is undervalued. Value it. Unappreciated. Appreciate it. Notice how sparkled you feel when you laugh – all of that energy cleansing.

And after you laugh and forget for a moment whatever you're binding too tightly, what's the first thing you do? Pull back to you? The same things you used to bother you before you laughed.

Que lastima. What a shame. Laughter clears out what bothers you and you move it immediately back in. Do so only if you choose. Or you can move in a better thought, a lighter mood, a more appropriate understanding.

Laughter chases away your blues, your chosen worries and sorrows. But then you feel guilty and call them back and put them back in place. Guilt is a glue you don't need. Make a choice. Glue this old thing back on again? Or let it go? If you glue it, make it your choice.

Laughter first. Invite laughter into your day.
(I lie on my back. Someone has come to show me what is in her carry. She takes out a clear attache case with a rhinestone shoulder strap, lowers it to a pile of clothes or blankets I have on the bed, indicating it's for me. Thank you. Oh, it's for holding the new book parts.)

February 14-15, 1999

Grace. What is grace but a laying aside of rules by which you bind yourself.

Grace is the suspension of that by which you punish yourself. We would advocate for more of this. It would improve your mood, lighten your heart. Be not so adamant imposing punishes and allow the space for grace.

February 15-16, 1999

Forgiveness is another way of love, giving blessing. Forgiveness echoes your heart thought with understanding, light. As you forgive, you connect your will with the cosmos/your will be done.

Imagine. There is nothing to forgive. Any thing you would forgive comes from a place of judgment. Forgiveness, then, is letting go of judgment. For who knows enough to judge? Who knows the larger purpose? Can see the highest good? Judging is a way of saying, I know how this should be. And this isn't it. Forgetting that how it is, is how it is to be. How it is is the material to create the next how-it-is and the next and the next. A rich blend of interaction which allows for growth and change. In setting a situation for forgiveness, you are in a situation of judgment. Notice this. Forgive – which means forgo judgment. Release judgment. Send unconditional love.

Forgive – which means release limitations you have put on yourself and others. When you have much to forgive, first forgive. It is a notice, a signal. Then look for the judgment and release the cause that called the need to forgive. When you have little to forgive, see you are releasing judgment. Ah. What greater good you serve by allowing yourself and others their paths.

Let forgiveness teach you to see each person in his dignity, his divinity, his right.

For when you allow each person his perfect right, forgiveness is no longer called for.

February 16-17, 1999

Awareness. Awareness is everything. Whatever you do with awareness is well done. Otherwise it's sloppy, not well-defined, a maybe. Be aware. Notice. Notice how each thing you do feels. Notice what you bring to it. Be aware how you allow it to affect you. Is it done with love? Is it done with consent? Or do you balk against it and do it because you feel you must. Acknowledge this. Not everything will change to love, automatically, but by noticing, you become aware of where love is and isn't.

Gently ask yourself, can I bring love there? Can I bring love there? And let it come where it will. Allow it. Encourage it.

Be aware. How does it feel when you let love come where it wasn't? What task is made lighter by letting in love? Notice where you put the blocks to lovingness. And notice how you hold them there. And when you notice, you will be able to make the choice, do I want it there? Do I want to let it go/can I let it go?

And make the choice. When love runs through what you do, you bathe yourself in love. You increase your energy. You are lighter. Notice. And make a choice. Do you do the things you do with love? Are you learning to do the things you do with love?

All is well.

Is that it? There's more. (Oh, it's for me.)

We wish to tell you, you are doing a good job. We wish you to be delighted with the book we are writing together and with what you're learning. Think not that you are making it up. We are. If it sounds like something you already know, it is because you are listening to all around you, because you tune in and learn. Nothing says you can't know what we're talking about for it to come from us. You're doing well and we are pleased. Thank you.

Thank you.

February 17-18, 1999

Jealousy – wanting what someone else has, not appreciating what you have. Jealousy is a why. A question you ask yourself. You know we would say appreciate. Know you draw to you exactly what you … (A deer comes to the almost dream place as I'm writing this. I stay as still as I can, stretched out here.)

June 11, 1999 (continued)
… know you draw to you exactly what is yours to experience.

Think not someone else's experience is better than yours, higher, fuller. Someone else's experience is different, only different. If you would draw to you other experience, examine what you send out as thoughts, as actions, as fears. For it is these which draw to you what you receive. (They're showing me/telling me/reminding me "Live by the sword; die by the sword.")

Your actions speak and your words speak and your thoughts speak, asking for what it is you receive. Clarify, then what it is you wish to receive. Use what you are receiving as an indicator of what you are drawing in. And make adjustments. Watch for changes. Acknowledge changes with gratitude and appreciation. As you make space for them by clearing unwanteds, the wanteds may come to you.

You have created. It is a way of showing thankfulness. So it is. Mirror yourself for you mirror god. This is so.

February 18, 1999
For someone

Brave Woman

I walk in light
I walk in truth
I forgive my misunderstandings
I allow others their choice
I align myself with courage
I lift my face to the stars

February 18-19, 1999

Calmity or calamity. Haven't you noticed how some people make a calamity out of every little thing, form a whirlwind of attention around themselves, the eye of the storm? Calm is hard to achieve too near these people. Always is the feeling of unsettling rushing wind. We do not mean excitement which is good and raises energy, but the type of distress that unsettles the balance and pulls you in where you don't want to go. Be aware. Be wary. And make your choice. If today you choose to be pulled into someone else's whirling energy pattern, hold onto your hat and step in. Be cautious. Be aware, though, of being pulled in without making this your choice. Whose energy will be whirling those winds once you step inside? No. First make your choice. And if you choose calm, sit down and wait it out. The whirlwind, the calamity will pass by. Without your consent, there is no interest for it here. The calamity isn't yours to solve, the winds not yours to settle. Sit down and hold peace with your whole self and feel just the breeze. You are smiling. It is good.

February 19-20, 1999

Trust. Are we talking tonight of trust? Putting yourself in the safekeeping of your own hands. Trust, though you may think it be in someone else, is, in actuality, in yourself. When you say, I trust that person, what really it is that you do is trust yourself and your all-knowing presence to have perceived this person in truth. Trust invokes harmony. Trust invites peace. Trust allows you to rest in your well-being. In trust is God. Trust acknowledges your connection with Source. Distrust does also. Discernment comes from trust, from acknowledging your connection. Discernment is the/allows you to/makes the distinction between trust and distrust.

This is confusing me. Can you make this so I understand it?

What's confusing you is the distrust.

Yes.

Let it go. Sleep on it. We will come back to this.

Did I get it all right for now?

Yes. You weren't confused. You'll see it's fine.
(Clarification as I read this over. Discernment allows you to make the distinction between trust and distrust.)

February 20-21, 1999

Sacredness. And what is sacred? When you wish upon a star and light from that star reaches you in a direct beam, and you notice it and honor it, that is sacredness.

Sacredness is seeing the sublime in the ordinary, the divine in what is. Sacredness is making room in your thoughts and beliefs for the recognition and reverence for the beingness of all that surrounds you. Sacred space is not something you make, create, set aside. Rather it is the recognition of what already is. You do not create sacred space. You honor it. You recognize it. You appreciate it.

When you see sacredness around you, you realize it is not a thing, but a way of being. Think not to name something sacred and set it aside from yourself. Rather include sacredness in every motion, every breath, every singing. As you send your thought to a star carrying a wish, and the star beams light to you, and you perceive this heavenly connection, so perceive the connection of sacredness and self. Thought goes out from you and beam comes back. Appreciate this connection. The harmony you feel with sacredness keeps it you, sets it not aside to be honored, but brings it to be honored within. And doing so, you will see the sacredness in you.

February 21-22, 1999

Faith. Steadfastness. Leap. Hold my hand. You are a child and I am a child. Faith is courage confirmed. Faith is the willingness to be led without knowing where you are going. Faith confirms inner knowing and arises from fear turned into trust. The fear that there is nothing there, the feeling I'm making this up. The hope that I'm not.

February 22-23, 1999

Steadfastness, holding steady to your purpose, being willing to stay on it no matter what. Steadfastness is the holy within you fulfilling obligations which you set for your greater good and the greater good of others. Like holding steady a rope so that you may count on it. Not letting it slack and become weak and undependable. The rope, when you hold it firm, can be trusted. When you don't, it goes slack, wobbles, skitters around. Hold your purpose with resolve and, like the rope, it is sturdy, dependable.

How will you know your purpose? You will know what makes you dance. Start there. What makes you sparkle. And when you trust your weight to it, it will hold you.

You cannot push the rope or pull it loosely and have it help you. Just so with your purpose. Your purpose holds firm in Source. And you need hold it taut and then you guide yourself along and stay on a true course.

February 24-25, 1999

Good morning. Love is everywhere. It is not something you have to create. It is. It is something you allow. When a tree stands with its eyes closed, reaching to the sun, it is love. When your cat comes to you for food, it is love. Love is. All things. We hear you say I love this. It is your expression of recognition. Not that you made up the love. But that you allow it.

Look in places where you do not feel love and you will see where you are blocking love. Yes. Other people block love and that sometimes affects you. But you take care of freeing love in you. Let them free love in them. As you free love in yourself, that will influence others. It is not your job to change others. They will change themselves. It is your job to free love. When others see that in you, something in them responds. But it is up to them to let it.

Watch the places in you that are stuck, held tight. Those are the places that you don't allow love. Those places in your body, your relationships, your attitudes, are telling you, "Let some love here." And when you let some love there, they stop being stuck, holding on, because they have what they needed. Watch for these places and listen wisely to what they teach you. It is enough.

All is well. So be it. Adieu.

Love is more than we have told you. More than we can tell you. It is the fabric of life, the web of light that connects you. It travels beyond your understanding. But let this much into your knowing and more will awaken. Love is the vibration and the vibrancy upon which all things depend. It has become a word for you, narrowly defined. Know it vaster than this.

Love exists with Source. Together with Source, unseparate from Source. Love is the vibrancy – which you call by many names – which keeps you alive in the world of the physical, alive in the world of the Spirit, alive in any dimension and level of being you can imagine. Love is the vibration. What gets in the way is not love. Clear that. Renew your connection and honor your being of Source.

All is love. Limit not your definition to specifics. Release the limitations that you place.

Then will you be rejoicing. Then will you find yourself in gladness. Love each part that tells you "this is not love" in body, relationships, attitude, so you may notice and love it and allow it to change.

February 24-25, 1999

Upholding justice not what we're to write on tonight.

Hail Mary, Full of Grace.

Grace?

Grace is given. But it must be received. If there is no reception for Grace, you don't perceive it around you, encircling you. Grace is given. Make of yourself a receiver of grace.

We hear you pray for grace when it is all around you. Like water, the ocean, for a fish, grace surrounds you so that you don't see it.
Grace abounds. Do not hold to it tightly but let it flow through you so that others may experience it in you and find it/recognize it for themselves.

As others see it in you, they recognize it for their own. They see whatever they do to hold it away and can change that. It is freely given and must be freely received. *Can* be freely received.

February 25-26, 1999

We're to talk of malice?

Malice is a pain that connects your heart with your heart. It is a beam you send outward which returns its barb to anchor your heart and weigh it down so it cannot move. See this as a sharp point and a strong weight. Hurtful thoughts go out, curve and re-enter, anchoring themselves in you. Awakening awareness of heart. Hurting. There are better ways to become aware.

Heaviness and soreness aren't the only way to bring your attention. Let's try love. Let's try appreciation.

February 26-27, 1999

Constancy. Pray remember. You are sometimes likely to set yourself in a direction and then forget about it. This does not get you where you want to go. This is the same as not steering your ship but letting it be pushed about by wind and waves. And then you wonder why you haven't arrived where you thought you were going. Set your destination. Invoke constancy – the remembering, the noticing/paying attention to your dream. Keep your hand on the rudder. Though you may be guided around difficult spots or directed to fortuitous opportunities, you still need your hand on the rudder to follow this guidance.

Set your star and, with awareness, with your action, keep yourself on a course headed toward it. If you be distracted by other things, think not to arrive where you first intended.

Stay alert. Remain interactive. Your goal is achieved.

Alarm. We would talk of undue alarm. This is not needed. Be not the one to go ringing catastrophes and dire news.

You surround yourself in gloom. Your brightness has trouble shining.

Feather off the clingingness of alarm thinking and open to light.

You do not keep what you fear away by ringing it. Instead you draw it to you. Be wary what you say in this bent and draw to you what you truly want.

Stimulate not others around you into thinking gloom for together you create much gloominess around you.

February 27-28, 1999

Sacred. We would teach you what you don't understand and remind you what you do understand.

Sacred is a trust. Sacred is a recognition of that which is holy within you and without you. Sacred is appropriate reverence and recognition and honor for that which is holy. Sacred is a placing of your holiness within the greater holiness, trusting to be recognized as well as to give recognition. Be bold in what you hold sacred. Be steadfast. The unwavering light. Sacred is not a setting aside but a setting within. So be it. All is well.

Fruition.

The coming into fullness, awareness of your godself comes as naturally from the blossom as fruit on a branch. Be not surprised that from the everything you are comes the awareness of being so. Now is the time. Be aware.

(I see Shilogh.)

Can you wait?

I can wait, he smiles, and I know he has been waiting like this, hands folded on his horse in front of him as he sits on the horse. He'll let me finish writing dreams.

Good morning, Shilogh. Thank you for waiting.

I am patient, he smiles, and urges his horse forward to be closer so we can speak. He slides down to the ground and from being bare-legged and barechested, he is now clothed in beautiful soft buckskin with a huge feather bonnet on his head.

Significance of this?

It is to show importance. (I bow my head to recognize this.)
It is important to remember who you are though you wear many different costumes. Important to know you are the son of god, offspring of the Great Being. You have important work to do, which you can do in many ways. Pay attention to what you are learning, for all of it is helping you. Look for signs, now, notices, to help you remember. All is well. The textbook is available. Pay attention. You can access what you need – as you have prayed.

"Ruminate" on this. Allow this to come into your conscious mind. The trying on costumes is great fun. No wonder you love it.

Portugal, yes, will be important. You don't have to work at it. Play fun and it will come to you as it is meant to.

Thank you.

(He inclines/nods his head to the horse.)

as I also thank you, horse.

(The horse lifts his head, so Shilogh mounts the horse.)
Remember, (he says and glides backwards with the horse to and into the forest edge.)

February 28-March 1, 1999

Physicality is the thickening of form. Physicality is more than the thickening of form. It is the vehicle which allows you interaction on the plane of cause and result. Beat not against this physicality which is yours – your gift to you. Beat in harmony with it. As your heart beats with the rhythm of the universe. For you are learning much from this. Be happy, joyous, with your discoveries and discover more. And more. As your awareness expands, so expands your possibility. Only you limit you. Learn this. All is well.

Each of you receives her own message as she listens. Each of you can learn from this. It is available. Know this. As you take the attention to ask and to listen, it comes. It is not ours to keep the silence, but yours to show willingness to hear.

March 1-2, 1999

Integrity? What is integrity but standing in your word. Use not your words loosely and stand surprised at the outcome. Your words are your word. Be clear in your meaning. Be clear in your words. Your words carry your power. If you would not put your power away from you, be careful with your words. If you would not use your power against yourself, be careful of your words. Maintain the power of your words. This is what is meant by integrity.

Choice is freedom. Even where there seems no choice, there is choice. Define your choices and you define yourself.

March 2-3, 1999

Bravery in the face of fear. Fear is not necessary. Let it go. Fear pushes from you what you most want/most need. Love fear. Honor fear for showing what is needed. When you recognize fear and its importance, it can get out of your way.

March 3-4, 1999

Peace is the laying-down of arms and armor; the laying-down of defenses which separate. Peace is a risk. In peace is its own reward. Lay aside anger and find peace. Lay aside stubbornness and find peace. Lay aside ill will and find peace.

Take your ministry where you will and in it find your peace.

You cannot find peace looking for it with arms and armor. Looking for it with expectations to be fulfilled, demands to be met.

Come to peace willing to set your will aside, and in the surrender to the highest good, find peace. Not you can orchestrate it except by releasing your grasp.

March 4-5, 1999

Peace. Be in fellowship with peace. Be in patience with peace. Think not to force it into being, but allow it to surround you. Interrupt not its calm with agitation; its quiet not with noise. For as you allow it to hold you, it holds you. All is well.

Peace lays its cloak around and enfolds you.

March 5-6, 1999

Anger is a way of not taking responsibility.

Anger is loneliness, aloneness. Hold anger to yourself and you hold off others. Is this what you want? So be it.

All is well with you, sugar. Yes. This writing is a testing, a practice, an adjusting to vibration. Be not discouraged, disappointed this is so. You have asked for this to be gently. And we are needing to adjust our own vibration to be so. Your willingness is all. You get to choose your project, your direction. This is as it should be. This is how it has been and how it will be. We are responsive, not directing.

What is it that is the most useful, uplifting, highest good? that I will love working with being part of? – also, a voice for writers.

A voice for writers:

We are not who you think we are. We are not talented. We are divine. We are not disciplined. We are divine. Who do you think we are? We are not. We are spirit living in truth with spirit.

How is it that the words come? In pictures? hearings? Translations of finer vibrations into print. What is it that we do? We leave our selves to travel. To observe and tell you.

What is a writer but the gatherer of energies, the focusser of thought, the brittle arranger of this is so.

You had it. It was easy. And you went beyond it. You had it, one day, sitting in the sunshine at the back corner of the house with words coming through your fingers to the keyboard of Mom's old typewriter. But it was too easy and your self stepped in and told you, I can do this better, make more sense than this. Let's try. And so you have been trying and succeeding. And now are ready to do without the try. This will be such fun, such enjoyment. A pulling together, culmination of all the separate moments of flying on words in other places. Oh, boy. Let's go.

March 6-7, 1999

Gratitude shows honor for what has been received and for what is. Gratitude quickens the heart, shines the connection, polishes it with light.

March 7-8, 1999 dreaming asleep

Let there be gladness on Earth whose time is coming. (At this point, I went off to build 7 buildings of grandeur.)

CHAPTER SEVEN

Enter now the holy space.
The temple that you are.

March 9-10, 1999. We leave for Portugal on the 10th

Good morning, Shilogh. Would you like to go to Portugal?

Of course, I'm going.

And your horse. (We nod at each other, look sideways at the horse, who pretends to be innocent.)

What's the horse's name?

Baby. (We nod. I think of "out of the mouths of babes" and the horse lifts his head, shows all his teeth, and whinnies.)

You will like Portugal. The people, the air, the flavor, the sunshine. Not all sunshine. Watch for things/events. They are coming. Here or there, the universe has heard you now, the sound of your voice and singing. Lift up your head and sing full strength.

All is well and all is changing. Just at the right time. You are ready. You are willing. You are able. Step into the new which is yours. People will help/you will be helped. You will be guided. Is it not so with us?

Yes. You do love flying (in a plane) except the noise. We'll see how to adjust that discomfort this trip. The "medicines" (remedy for jet lag) are fine and safe to take and will help you to stay sparkling, as they promise. With ease you will make the transitions from here to there and there to here. You are good at this and do it well. You have had lots of practice. (Sleep/wake, travel, etc.)

(Comment: Noise bothered me less and both transitions were easy.)

March 12-13, 1999 Lisbon, Portugal, dreaming asleep

> Man signs our orders again and they beam light. I knew this would happen as I'd told our group, "Have him sign the orders and they become light – not heavy." (I wake.)
>
> Before this I'd had him sign our orders which were rolls of paper. He is a Master and yet he does as I suggest, I note. We are working together. I am leader of our team. Others have their orders signed when I suggest it.
>
> Also: There's a slot – we're leaning for our angel to come through. Someone shifts a template.

Dreaming awake

> Many beings, an entourage – ready and willing to help? Yes.
>
> As I'm giving thanks, a helmet is fitted over my head. The kind with a nose piece like Greek or Trojan. And I'm given a long, wide, sword into my right hand. The being who gives me these is a man, slightly taller than I, who wears a long, gilded and embroidered stiff cape and a sword. He is balding at top of head. I do not kneel or bow, but man-to-man stand and accept these. It seems an action on my way to something else where I will need these. I bow my head in respect and thanks and move past him.

Dreaming asleep

> "The metropolis sent us," I hear, "to be guided here."
>
> Now I see a great, mighty being with wings on his helmet. And I think of Hermes, the messenger god.

Do you have a message for me?

Yes. You come from aeons, from planets, from suns. You are not who you think you are this time, but vastly more powerful by far than you can even imagine. When you remember this, truly remember, the way will be smooth and light and you will see it always has been. (I see me helping others understand this. I have my arm around someone – I have wings on my hat/helmet and so do the others – helping him/her (no gender) upwards. Others are around, following. I see this as over the shoulder of the guide with the helmet and wings. See all of us streaming upwards toward him. As if I'm leading and others broaden in a curve behind me. He is smiling, welcoming.)

Yes. We are happy to greet you, Sister. We have waited to greet you face-to-face and let you know how well you are doing. (There is one place I come through. Like a space in space, and he's there as a guide so I know where we will all pass through. It is not a gate or doorway, but a certain space surrounded by space. All is light as in a painting of angels moving upwards. Reminds me of angels – upwards.)

Yes. You are beings of Light. We are beings of light. It is all the same. We greet you as ourselves. (How beautiful. I see us all still, as in a painting, not moving. And now see us from behind me. I have stumbled through, pulling the someone with me. She seems an old woman now with loose curls of gray hair under her helmet.)

Thank you for this vision and truth.

All is well. You are deeply loved. And you have plenty of paper for these writings. You will sleep if you like. Enough for now. (See green light as if a mist falling from horizontal line. As I return to unity mudra, (hand position for Melchizedek meditation) there's a puckering in my solar plexus that is very real.)
"I am with you and I am God," I hear as I return.

Later, grizzly bear comes and stands large to my left.

Asleep dreaming
　　Our universal oneself finds itself suspended in a hologram near the ceiling of a large, tall room. Before this I saw me to the side, being given a new paradigm, and hearing the words, "You are being given a new paradigm."

Awake dreaming

　　"I am ready to feed you," a god tells me, reaches things from a counter/slot to place onto the tray/plate that appeared in my hands. I was given this tray of food which now the god adds to. Light appears on the tray also. "This is my food for you," the god says. "Manna."

Thank you. (I bow my head, the tray in both hands. He smiles.)

Awake dreaming

"I know what your game is and I'm mad," I speak. I see feet in white socks. The canvas type shoe I have, but in navy blue.

To whom am I speaking?

The gods. You're angry at not being let in on the game sooner, but this could not be. You know this could not be, but you do like being in charge/control/making your own decisions.

Be patient. Be calm. Everything comes to you. Let it. Allow it to unfold – like the mandala is many petals, forms, layers, folding/unfolding into others. You will like this.

Be assured. All is well and as it "should" be. Delight in what is. Revel. It is yours. (I see John ask about last night's writing. "I wrote volumes in the light of God," I answer.)

Dreaming asleep

"What's most important to you?" angel asks.
That you feel hugged.
(I hug angel so she'll feel hugged. She hugs me so gently I feel transported.)

(A gold fabric vest with sheer white sleeve/wings is being put onto me now.)

March 14-15, 1999 in Obidos, Portugal dreaming asleep

"What are you doing now?" someone asks.
"Grounding light into the planet." I see me walking down the steps of some huge amphitheatre. It is dark but light shines on my face and on the faces of others, as if firelight or so. We look

rather like faces of light, flames of candles, moving down the stairs. I remember a dream of angels in a line into the distance – that in the distance looked like candle flames.

Awake dreaming

Now I see a woman angel seated on the top stone step in the doorway of a cathedral? Or church? Plain stone arch with doors behind it, closed. She has a book open to her right on the step and her knees pointed toward it, a large size book, but not thick. One of the pages stands up as if turning. She is not looking at the book, though. She is looking off, waiting. The book is to look at as she's waiting. But she's not reading it. She looks a little sad. She looks now like the Mucha girls or so, large eyes, hair softly up, brown in color. I wish her well. She seems to brighten as if with hope.

March 16-17, 1999 Bussaco, Portugal

Good morning, Shilogh. Are you here?

I am here.

In Portugal?

In everywhere. Don't be surprised. It is a wonderful/marvelous horse. (He nods and smiles. I am smiling.)

Do you have something to tell me?

Do you have something to tell me?

Yes. I have been learning lots. In dreams. It is wondrous. Delightful.

Yes. Because you are there.

I dreamed angel Michael came and I was in a group.

It is because you wish to learn that you go to these places. It is quite wonderful, no?

Yes. It is.

Be willing. All that is necessary is that you be willing to learn. And you are.

Thank you.

You're welcome. You're not asking if you're on the right path? You are.

Thank you.

'Brigado. (Means thank you in Portuguese.)
(You speak languages, I gesture. It's the horse, he gestures.)

(I see a large snake twining, changing shape of the figures he makes and hear:)
"There are still other ways to do it if we didn't do it this way, this space, this time."

March 17-18, 1999 Marvao, Portugal
Awake dreaming

You have not found all.

So I'll keep going?

Yes. You are looking for light. Keep going. Keep aware. All is well. This is a magnificent time of growing. Don't work at it. Be aware. Be present.

March 23-24, 1999 dreaming asleep

This is my Christ vestment.

Dreaming awake

Bring yourself joy. Bring yourself happiness. Bring yourself the things you want and need. They are yours already. You just need let them in. Open the door so they arrive. This is a glorious time. Revel in it. Delight. These times are yours. Don't be tied to old ways. Find the new ways. Let go. Let God take you places you want to be.

All is well. All is truly well. Fly with it. Glide. You're making so much work. Relax and glide. Your work is done/is being accomplished. Rejoice. Don't you see the ease with which things come? All things are yours. Breathe in them. Live. Be alive the way you know how to be.

This occasion is joyous. Everlasting. Be revived. The sparkle that is you is needed by others. Is accepted and adored. Revel in this. Let the other go.

"Believe in the Christ in you," I tell someone at tai chi.

March 27-28, 1999
I see the upside-down face of a wolf looking at me. Some brown as well as gray fur.

Good morning, Wolf. Do you wish to speak? Do you have a message?

You are deeply loved. Whatever may transpire today, know that you are loved, that it is proper and appropriate that you be so. That your intent is a good intent. You are fragile/not fragile. You are tougher than cord. You have the right to make your own decisions. It is what you're here for. Relax your vigilance in this circle, but allow what things you choose. It is fine to be open. You are protected. But in openness, you choose.

Thank you, Wolf.

Thank you. ("I am a Spiritual Being wearing wolf's clothing," I see/hear.)

March 28, 1999

We are your starry family and we are proud of you. It is wonderful to watch how you follow suggestion lately and find you are channeling from us. We are happy to be recognized in your work – the work we do together.

Are these the beings I was meeting up the runway of light?

Yes. (They are exultant at being recognized. I am so happy. They form a large circle. I am part of the circle. They are cheering. They are celebrating that I've finally met them on a conscious level and it makes such sense to me.)

Is the channeled writing I'm to do different from what I've been doing? No.

I'm already doing this? Yes.

> I'm channeling from my soul family. This is so awesome. I can see them. They're delighted I can see them. (energy chills and tears) They're celebrating. Well, they've been waiting for me to recognize them and now are pleased.
>
> I speak in gratitude to my soul family; to whatever wisdom got me here. I feel in my solar plexus the seed of what's to come. I see banners. I remember banners above and surrounding dear Mother Earth which I could see from a distance.
>
> Banners above the planet. Banners extending. I see the earth, the banners above it, around it.
>
> I speak in gratitude to my true self for protecting when I need protecting, guiding when I need guiding, and revealing herself when I need to see her.

> You are part of a family of souls – inner beings – who resonate at the same frequency. They're non-physical beings – same harmony and purpose.

> Who do you think has been helping you?

Am I ready now? To understand and do it?

Yes! You're ready now.

March 28-29 waking

Are we to write now?

Sit when you get to your room.

Please remind me. You are welcome here. – I mean in my life.

But suddenly, they're here. (My starry family) Stream of light of all of them into my body. I see them all individuals again inside, feeling the container of my body with their hands, looking out. Lots of motion, running from one place to the next in my body like exuberant children. Excited. I'm smiling.

March 29, 1999 evening, I dance.

God: So you've found your family.

Yes. Or they've found me.

They've been searching for a long time. They have wanted you to know on a conscious level. As you have wanted to know, know that all energy serves and all is well. There is not a way for you on earth to not achieve what you have begun.

I see my whole family now, getting up from the circle to come and hug me (goosebumps), make much of me. You are very loved, they seem to be saying.

We <u>are</u> saying. And very much honored.

Their brightness is transferred to me. I think, I can <u>live</u> in this brightness. They're (goosebumps) smiling, nodding, yes, you can. I see me float from the center of the circle, still in sparkles of light, drift down to walk on the earth. There are ribbons floating also as if to connect me in a flowing-ribbons way. The space does not close but stays open. I am welcome there. You are welcome here. Someone flits down – like a curious child or tinkerbell faery and flits around and goes back. I see this as if watching them and me. There's a ringing in my ears.

March 29-30, 1999
(I hear my soul family)

We are pleased, very pleased, that you recognize us now. (Lying down for sleep, I felt a touch on the back of my right/write hand.)

This will be easy. Easier now. You will see. Joyous. Like dancing.

Stay focussed with us a few moments and let's see what happens. Stay curious. You are gaining recognition of our selfs and your self. It is right that you want to know, that you ask, and are learning. You will make the right choices always.

All is well. You will see how smoothly we go. There is a garden. You know nothing yet of the garden. Now go inside and look. Tell what you see.

The air that lifts off the garden is moist and cool, holding dusk inside it, ending of a day. The light is quiet light. Nothing intrudes on the sanctuary of this place.

Enter now the holy space. The temple that you are. Allow now the first fireflies to blink in the smoothness of the gloaming. Breathe in the sanctity and the reverence that is here. And as you breathe, drift. Allow yourself to glide and come loose from your own beliefs which hold you standing in one time, one place.

Allow yourself to drift like currents of air, like ribbons on the wind. Allow yourself to lift and soar and glide. And as you allow yourself this freedom, unloose from expectations. Unloose from your history. Play on the currents that lift you. Look down on the world below. Notice the garden. See yourself in the garden in the pose in which you left you there. See that you are safe there. Protected, guided. Secure. And turn your self to the sound you are hearing now, high above the earth. Describe it so you can remember and take it back with you. Notice it with all your attention. Let the bounce describe you. Let the wave curl onto itself. And stay curious. And be the wave that lifts and curves and shatters into itself. (I see the face of a man. The forehead rises into a crown. ¾ profile view.)

On a stream of light energy project yourself into the model of your person. On a beam of light, bring yourself into your body in the garden. And open your eyes and remain aware.

March 31, 1999 morning meditation

I see my starry soul family and a runway of light I saw in a dream last year and the tall noble beings in rosy light there.

Yes. Those are the Wisdom Masters. We go to them to know things.

April 1-2, 1999
Shilogh

You're doing very well, dear one, dearest. Very well, indeed. Now you have us on a journey and we wonder where we'll go. Anywhere. Anywhere you'd like to take us. We'll come along because we're adventurous. And sturdy of heart.
(I see my starry family in their circle. They're moving around as if at a camp, doing what needs to be done and taking their ease while we're not writing – oh, it's sort of – doing the things I'll do in between – but knowing it's the writing that's important.)

Yes. They're pleased. And they know you've just begun. This is your journey, too.

Thank you. Thank you, horse. (He's here over Shilogh's right shoulder.)

April 2, 1999 meditation

We want you to know you are loved and you are honored. We honor you. (This is in the rosy light.) We honor you your courage, your strength, the time you have taken to put yourself in the place of receiving. Wisdom. Words. Starry essence.

I honor you your patience, your wisdom, for allowing me into your space and welcoming me with gladness.

There is much to do and we have made good beginnings. It is for us all to discover what story goes forth from here. That is to say it isn't written. It is being written with you.

It comes from a place of unknowing into a place you will know. Such is creativity born in the world.

Let us hold you, then, as you write the words that come to your heart. Let us serve you as you serve us with your pen.

Yes. May I accept this.

It is yours. (They make a big fuss over me, playing me dress-up, which I love. Some sort of veil and long dress and wreathed around in swirling colors. This I can accept because to me it's fun.)

We are to play – to costume. To drink tea. Tea party. And somersaults. And flying. Astound me now. Astound me. I am ready. To be overjoyed.

> Whoop. There is the hammock and I'm bouncing. With Kwan Yin, Jesus, Mary, bear looking on. Oh. Now the starry family is with them. Has joined the rosy circle. Oh. I see the veil and gown of my divine self.

April 8-9, 1999

> Sacrifice. Sacri – heart.
> I sacrificed my heart. Oh. In choosing to be the one whose heart was cut out and offered to the gods rather than the priest who cut it out (dream some years ago).

Sacrifice – the giving up of heart. The releasing of what you hold most dear. Creating the hollow, the space for god to reside. The readiness to know your purpose and accept it. The eagerness to get on. The giving up to highest good. Giving up heart to find it, and to let good presence fill you.

April 9-10, 1999

> Now I'm with the beings in the rosy light. But not among them. As if peeking over some edge at them. It seems like upstairs in the barn when I was little.
> "We want to abandon you," they're saying. I can't quite see over the edge. I wonder why but I don't feel fear. Now, writing, it is, "We won't abandon you." Yes. This is accurate.

We won't abandon you. For you are important to us. More important than you know. For your courage and wisdom and well-being (being stable is necessary to do this effectively). We have provided material. It is well used. We will provide more. And the guidance to use it. Fear not. You are always protected, guided, and safe, no matter what it looks like around you. Let yourself know ease. Let yourself be merry/Mary? Yes both. It is so with you. Relax into it. Let it hold you. Yes. Like the hammock. Let it give you rest to know we hold you and you hold us. Even as you are discovering, your angelhood, your humanness are helping us. Necessary to us. Important to us. Great things can be/are being accomplished by this stitching together of layers. (Image yesterday as we channeled light to the light beings – stitching together, bringing angels and humans together in helping each other.)

These are important times. Changing times. And you are part of the change. A leader in the change. One many will listen to and hear because of your true message. Now is a time to put faith in your connection to Source and know it to be strong. Now it is safe to do that. And needed. And wanted. Now is a time to tell others, to show them with your work and with your words. As you write of this, speak of this, those who will hear you listen. And it is strong. And sturdy. This connection. And holds. Supports. Keeps glowing with intensity. Now is a time to act in knowledge of your own doing. All is well with us. And with the world. Don't worry about the specifics of your time. Concentrate and meditate on bringing in the light, which has consequences past what you can imagine. All is well. All is well.

Sleep well. Sleep in peace. We are here. We want to help you as you want to help us. Rest now and remember. Remember. Remember yourself. Your beautiful starry self. Good night.

April 12, 1999

You know the answer is love, but don't know what love includes. A variety of styles for new behavior.

April 14, 1999 morning (I see me wearing a gold dress and speaking/ teaching this.)

There is to be a new learning, each to her own. There is to be a style of living in which peace abounds. Yes. It is possible. It is on its way. As you make the path straight, it comes.

Think not how things have been. They can be like that no more. The vibration of this planet and all among it changes – is being changed – by you and others like you who hold the seed and the crystal of the new.

Ho, as you hold and cherish the light – which is information, learning, do you make it bright and shine it and the world is changed by you.

Think not, I must do this, or I must learn how. The doing is in you now. The knowing is in you now. Your willingness directs it. Your willingness allows to happen the changes which you bring.

Is this true speech from the greatest wisdom? Yes.

You have a way to check this now and test its truth. It is good. Be you at peace. As you ask, we answer.

As the new vibration comes in, there is wanting people to guide it, to guide the world, to guide her peoples. And you are the guides, the ones people will turn to.

Easy it will be to accept this and take authority and use it. Be not lulled into thinking this is the way. Instead, do as you have been doing. Guide and allow each her learning. For not only you are important. But everyone is important. Yes. Each her own authority with guidance and guided wisdom. Let the love in your heart lead you and so lead others. To their own brilliance.

We're counting on you.

April 15-16,1999 dreaming asleep

Our image of the world needs to change.
We need to understand the things these stories can teach us, I'm saying about the books in print.

April 17-18, 1999
Shilogh

I see you at the forest edge. I see you cover your face and peek at me. What is this brightness? you seem to say with raised eyebrow and squintings. Am I that bright? Is it me you see shining?

Yea, are you bright. Unto the heavens is your brightness. Truly you are discovering your own. And bringing it forth.
It makes us glad to see it. (I see his horse is there. The horse, Baby, also shies away his head. They seem to find this very amusing.)
You are with god. With godness all about you.

Is this true?

It is true. Believe it of yourself for it is so. Truly, you shine forth that others may see you. Know you not, this is so?
Yea. Verily. For you are meant to be much in this time/place. You are truly meant to lead. In creativity. In thought. In spiritual awakening. You have placed yourself well for what you are about. Take yourself kindly. As do others.
In standing your truth you are not always liked, but always you are loved. If there be a falling away of that which can't keep up with you, let there be a falling away. So that you may proceed unfettered. And unfetter others. So it will be.
As you set your intent, it answers. As you ask, you shall be served. Multitudes are wanting to help your intent. See yourself as a crystal taking form. And take form in/as the shape and color you choose to be.
Even now, as a crystal, you reflect the light that we may see you.
(I have a carrot for Baby and for Shilogh I have a hug. He is all hard edges, not accustomed, it seems, to hugs.) We'll meet again.

Ho. And thank you.

April 19, 1999 afternoon, writing room

Now, be at peace. Now look forward as never before. As your gifts are illumined, you take them from the cabinet and make of them good use.

Self-actualization is big. Very big. You are not aware of some (gifts). Of some, you are. As days pass, you become more and more of who you are. You accept into your reality more of who you can be. Direct your attention now to using your gifts, which are yours to use. All you need do is listen and it comes. All you need do is write and it is there.

Everything has its purpose as you have your own. All is well in this. You would not be guided in ways not beneficial. Listen to your guidance. It is you who honor yourself. Revel in this. It is time for revelation.

Stand with us as we work/play. Stand with us and be glad.

The definitions?

They have their place separate from here yet connected. All will be given. All guidance. All direction. Do not fret. Already is it in place and coming to/toward you.

There is more. This is what you call a charmed circle. This circle of our being. Much are we together with you. And much are you together with us. And so we increase each other. And so we prosper in purpose. And so is much good done.

Truly you are sent of god. And truly you return. And so you stand in your truth and teach others. (Goosebumps. Tears. Sobs.)

I am ready to begin (test no, I have already begun.) *You will please come again and tell my readers what they need to know?* Yes.

These are changing times and humans need to change with them. The animal and plant and mineral kingdoms are also receiving advice on change. This advice may take the form of a book as a book is in your knowing. A book can be opened by the hands of humans and held in the lap and understood in the heart. A book is a way of power. For where there is understanding at the heart/soul level, understanding empowers, brings power. In this case, power to choose and power to change.

April 19-20, 1999 ~

We are here. We are ready when you are. What would you know?

Some information, please, to go into the books – and which book.

We proceed.

Love is an answer and love is the question. Whether, as a species, you can live in the frequency of love. Many of you there are holding the love vibration and many are to come. But in the meantime, is the frustration and impatience surrounding those who do not see. From your new/heightened perspective, it is easy to ask why can't they get it? But they can't get it the same as you couldn't get it before you were here. Let it then be your task to hold the vibration purely without judgment that much love may come through you and change the world.

This is a way of being. This matters. This counts. This is what it is that is changing the world. Value yourself that you perceive it. Value others that they are willing to learn. Someone must lead and set the intention and keep it firm. Allow others their perceptions and keep steady your own and from this are you learning, as well. From this you teach without teaching. All is well.

April 20, 1999 afternoon meditation

There is much to be learned here, and you, as a knower, bring much to the planet. Energies, reserves, consciousness, awareness, more than you know. Revel, we have said. For this is revelation. We are coming to this smoothly, softly, to be not misunderstood. There is such light around you that you invite the energies for highest good. And we invite you, as well.

Take off, for the moment, all official costumes. Come and play with us at dress-up. And see what can be. Within you and outside of you. Delight as, carefully, we brighten the intensities and color. Yes. How does it feel walking just a bit above the earth?

We are going to be talking of healing. And of writing, also. And then you are going to choose how this goes together or stands apart.

You are going to use it as you use experience for your stories. Does this go here? Or should it be saved to make another story? You will know. You will see. It will delight you.

You are small to go into small places, to fit between the worlds and to make of your gatherings a fine piece that some will understand. To illumine, in ways you are used to, those things which need to be said.

All is well. We are progressing. We are together in this.
The meditation for writing is an excellent way to step into another world. We like it and others will follow. You listen well. We listen.

Ask us questions if you like.

Please provide help in my asking the questions?

Of course. Many are needing to connect with their creative selves. Set the seeds for how to do this and people will respond.

April 21, 1999 invocation, morning

Good morning.

We are with you now. What would you know?

Can you tell me about religions?

Believe in your own knowing. Believe not in your beliefs, but challenge them and challenge them until you come to your own knowing. It is that when you discover a belief that is not your own knowing, that comes from someone else, perhaps as a gift, perhaps as a loan, you can return it now to the giver. So it does no longer affect you. See yourself doing this. If it is not your own knowing, see you holding the gift of religion or the gift of cautiousness over money or the gift of not trusting strangers. See you holding the gift – as you have wrapped it beautifully – out to the giver of that belief and smiling and saying thank you as you return it. And as many people as gave you the gift may receive it back from you. Think of the belief and of whom it came from and return it to all the whoms.

Become aware of another belief. Test if it is truth with you. If it is not, if it is limiting, think of who gave you the gift. With gratitude for what it has taught you, return the gift in your mind's pictures.

As you notice beliefs which are not truths, as you show your willingness to give them back, these beliefs clear from your field and no longer limit you. And, also, in clearing, make space for truth you invite to enter. So it is.

And what of the collective? Of people who gather/come together?

Let people come together in truth, in awareness, which is light. Not in conclaves to further the beliefs which limit. When it happens that because of going to a church or holy site, or reading a holy scripture, someone experiences upliftment, then is it that that person has broken through the confinement and accessed his own greater truth. And one does not need religion to do this. One does not need a collective.

Something more on religion?

Not at this time. You understand.

Yes. Thank you.

CHAPTER EIGHT

You must understand the Beloved is you. And also, you must not forget this.

April 23, 1999 I lead a meditation at a circle of friends

We invite you to pause and shift and center and leave outside the room whatever of the world you came through to get here to this safe place. And notice in your body, any place of tightness and let it go, creating space. Check your neck and shoulders, chest and ribs and back, knees and calves.

We invoke our guides, spirit helpers, angels, energies, beings of light which guide us and protect us and keep us safe. We acknowledge our ancestors in the biological and spiritual lineage with gratitude for our being here in this moment, in this space.

And I invite you to allow the energies to hold you for the next few moments as we ask to access all levels of wisdom – wisdom of the conscious mind, unconscious mind, the great beyond, and the wisdom of our life force energy, recognizing that although we may think we are separate, we are one.

And I invite you now to notice your breath. And notice that on the in-breath you can draw fresh clear energy into your body and that on the out-breath you can release any stress or tension. And as you breathe in, you may begin to notice that you can draw energy from the earth up through the soles of your feet and you can release any tensions as you breathe out. And as you breathe in, draw the energy up your legs and feel it brighten, turning on the light in you, in your beautiful light body. And as you breathe out, release any blocks, creating space for energy on the in-breath to come up your body and into the solar plexus. And on the next breath, into the heart.

And feel the energy expand your chest and break up patterns of old emotions you no longer need, so you can release them on the out-breath and draw clear energy from dear mother earth to fill the space of your heart. And draw the energy to your throat chakra. And release. And draw the energy to the third eye. And up to the crown of your head. And as you feel the energy at the crown of your head, you may begin to notice that on the in-breath you can draw energy from the heavens into the crown of your head.

And into the third eye chakra, filling space that you've made to receive it. And into the throat chakra. And into the heart. And into the solar plexus. And sparkling down the legs to the ankles and feet.

So that you recognize yourself now as a bridge of light between heaven and earth, the rainbow bridge, grounding light to the planet.

And as you stay in this space you have created for the next few moments, you might invite the wisdom of your body to show you anything it would like you to know. Anything that would like your attention. It may be a word or an image or a feeling. And give it your attention.

And you might want to ask this word or image: What would you like me to know? Or, How is it you serve me?

And listen and observe, allowing space for an answer to come. And when you have done this, give yourself a few moments to carry on a dialogue or to receive a learning or to perform, in your imagination, whatever action seems appropriate. And do that now.

And when that feels complete, in whatever way seems appropriate, express gratitude for this learning and bring the meditation to a close, honoring yourself and your wisdom and your learnings.

And begin to come gently back to the room, bringing with you, on a conscious level, what it is you've learned.

I invite you to remember who you are as you gently come back to this space.

And find yourself in the room with the light around you that others may see your light.

And smiling to yourself and to others, open your eyes to let us know you're back.

April 24-25, 1999 ~

And what is sex but a pathway for yourself to encounter yourself. A covenant of energies fulfilling energies. A conduit of divine intelligence into your awareness.

How is this so? Through trust. And awakening. Not through hiding. Not through not knowing who you are. Or pretending not to. Through the vibrancy which comes with being aware. Do not speak in darkness. Speak in light. And let light fill the spaces you hold for it.

What is sex? The attunement of energies. Of two people. The attunement of energies can lift or flatten. Rise the spiral or descend. Watch for this. You will find it. Much can be gained or lost. And the attunement also with source. The frequency you blend on. The frequency you send out and allow in. Where you blend with another's essence, allow the blending to teach you, to inform.

April 24-25, 1999 dreaming asleep

I'm singing the essence of the daffodil. There is the feeling of daffodils in the air. I'm sitting with my eyes closed, palms up, receiving, breathing essence of the daffodil, hearing the song of the daffodil without words.

April 27, 1999

You know the most important thing is love, but you don't know what is included in love.

April 28, 1999 morning, invocation

Are you ready? Here we go.

Speak when you are comfortable speaking. It is not necessary to speak before. It is not necessary to play the game on the world's time. Play the game on your own. Create the time necessary for you. All is already given. Relax and allow the sweetness, the goodness, the ripeness of this "Now."

For as you participate in the sweetness of now, you expand it, allow it to be seen by others who must see it to understand.

Hold the sweetness for others to taste. That is just what you are doing. And it is important. And it matters. All is one. And as you hold the sweetness for others, it is returned to you.

Many times over is it expanded then, sweetening the world, expanding the consciousness so sweetness may be known.

May 2-3, 1999

You know love, whereof it is made.

May 3-4, 1999 ~
For someone

Fear is being stepped up as promised. Fear not. Act not from fear but from love. Know that everything changes and all is well within that. Nothing you can do can rock the security, the safety, the serenity, you can feel when you allow yourself to feel it. Fear is external. Love always within. Trust the love within you, which is divine. Trust yourself to make mistakes and right choices. And love yourself through them. Look not outside yourself for love that is within you. Find it in the core and fibers of you and you find it else. Fear not that this is true.

Yes. Very great learning now for the foundations have cracked and allow in light. (I see this as the kind of light that we can see in rays through clouds shining into cracks in stone and filling the places – the way you see light in fog – that misty magic glowing shining that has no edges.)

The connection to God is direct. It can be counted on. Because we need to know this, we will know this through whatever times it takes. Because love *is*.

Look in yourself for love. And the external will reflect you. This is so.

Farewell, Abide, Adieu.

May 11-12, 1999

I am thinking the name, St. Germaine. Do I have a connection?

Yes.

Will you help now?

I am helping.

Are you channeling some of the information? Yes.

All of the information? Yes.

Shilogh? Yes.

Is there something else for me to know?

You are loved. Deeply loved. How could it not be so? What else would you know?

That which is for my highest good to know now and that which is for the collective.

Your books will soar because truly they contain wisdom, the wisdom the world is waiting for, thirsty for, ready to accept. You will see. Be at ease with this. All will come smoothly. It will be so because I am St. Germaine. Yes. You are meant to know this now. It's fine. Rest. It is true you need rest now. And also true you work hard in your resting. You rest to good purpose – for yourself and others. Your way is made clear. Go out. This is not the you, the *lesser* you, but you, the greater you. Shine in that brilliance that is yours to shine. You are protected. All is well. The hour comes and now is for you to fulfill your blueprint as ordained.

Thank you.

Adieu.

May 11-12, 1999 ~

Katherine is of the highest order. Yes. A very winged being.

May 12-13, 1999 ~ (One of my students has told me about violence at a school in Colorado. I hear "Littleton needs you." I send distant healing. Gather people.)

Prayer for Littleton, meditation:

Go inside and find the still place. The place that though everything around it be quaking, holds still and calm – and breathe this. Find the place that cannot forgive and ask it to forgive as you would ask/want forgiveness for *your* children had it been the other way around.

And when you balk or begin to think, go back to that still place and breathe. And from that still center, ask the unforgiving place to forgive.

Because of your earnestness, your sincerity in examining yourselves, a major war is averted. Already the soldiers are on bivouac. They expect the night bombs to come screaming in. They wait in fear and discomfort. And as you assess yourselves and as you change your hearts from asking why to forgiving, in the place of war, nothing happens. As you change your hearts, soldiers lay down their guns and can sleep. The war goes past us for this time.

When you question why this had to be, if it had to be, go to the still place. The questions are your notice that you've stepped out of your center. Step back in and breathe. And ask the unforgiving place to forgive. And ask forgiveness for yourself – for anything you may wish to have done differently. For anything you'd like to take back. Take it back now. And change it. And release it with love.

And breathe in the still place, without judgment, without thought. Breathe in the knowing there is nothing to forgive. And from that still center, start to notice, to feel the love you feel. Feel it inside you and feel how it expands around you – and expands. And notice you can feel love from others in the room. Maybe those beside you or those across the room. And as you notice this, your love brightens stronger. Let it brighten. Let it shine to encompass the whole room.

And others are shining with you. And notice that. And accept how that feels in every cell of your being. Breathe in love and breathe out. And allow any doubts to be surrounded in love. They don't have to be resolved. They only need to be loved. And as you notice them, any time, surround them in love and allow them. Not with resistance, with love. You are changing your heart to this purpose – to love.

And from the vast amount of love you have generated in the room, bring back some now to your heart, that you receive. And breathe. And breathe.

And as you prepare to come back to this time and this place, bring with you the experience of your heart so that always your heart reminds you, informs you this is so.

And as you bring yourself back gently, you'll notice the light in the room, and you may see that someone near you needs your hand. And someone on the other side, as well.

May 14, 1999

There is a thoughtform on earth now. And that thoughtform is love. Take it where it takes you. Let yourself trust, not the specific love, but the greater love. For in trusting the greater love, you bring the specific into being.

There is a new thoughtform on earth. Different in magnitude than what has been before. Some there have been who carried this wave form and others found it in *them*, but not in themselves. Now is the time we find it in ourselves.

For then, we honored the vessel that brought it and not the learning, made much of the bringer into religions and gods.

But now is the time we honor what was taught and lost or placed aside.

There is a new thoughtform on earth now and we are here to know it in ourselves. And by our knowing it, the love thought will spread and others will know it also. You have been here many times and you have yearned for this time when it is appropriate to be known for this waveform/this vibration. When it is safe to know it and let it shine forth.

Truly it is a remarkable time and you will be glad to be in it. You will be glad to be shining. And at your peace.

There is nothing for you to do or say. Acknowledge yourself and hold the light and watch how you change the world.

All is well. Be blessed.

May 23-24, 1999 ~
Shilogh

You're doing fine. Nothing is to worry about. You are being more and more and more spiritually guided and this is good for you. To get out of your own way. To allow. To listen. Good and good and good. Maybe you don't notice me now because I am with you always. Instead of a "meeting" there is a flowing. I still like "meeting" like this. It is a stopping to notice. But/And also, the stopping/holding still to notice isn't necessary when the flowing together is there. Be calm and energetic. Things are coming to you in all the right ways. You have been setting up for this and we have helped.

Thank you.

Yes. You are welcome. It is experience.

I remember being blissful about the dreams. I just don't remember them.

Bliss is pretty nice, huh? And the purpose of some dreams. You travel to far-off places. Remember whatever you can. But don't worry about what you don't. It will come again or it is stored with you in ways you don't need to remember consciously. Build a reservoir of bliss. What could be better? (I see him now at the edge of the woods, standing with the horse, Babe, who rolls her head and tells me, Hello.)

Hello, Babe. (Which I think means good-bye as they fade backwards into the woods.)

Thank you for coming.

(He warbles something with his hand over his mouth and mounts the horse.)

Namaste.

(I can smell sweet smoke of something burning. Not incense. Campfire or sage or so.)

May 27-28, 1999

You must understand the beloved is you. And also, you must not forget this.

May 27-28, 1999 ~

Ah, is it different names I'm called? Yes.

The works of fiction, Randeane.
The works of channeling et al.

Thank you. It makes so much "sense" now. And oh – how lovely that I can give credit now. This is How I can give credit! (tears) Thank you, loved ones. It has been bothering me since my greater understanding, to take credit for your work.

Always take credit. We want it so.

You do?

Yes! (Muscle tests yes.) We work *with*, not without you.

This is it? Yes.

Thank you for making me more and more attuned/ comfortable with what we're doing.

May 31-June 1, 1999 ~

Your books are all around you. Choose what you'd like. (When I heard this, I began to have an idea of the non-separation of what is personal and what is for the highest good of the collective.)

May 31-June 1, 1999 ~

Hello. (Such a musical feminine voice.)

Hello.

We are here to guide you so you don't be lonely in this book. All is well. The knee is well. Be happy/joyous in this work/play. Worry not how this will go together as we will be folding things with you. The book folds together so beautifully – you will see. This one done and on to the next one. We're writing the next one and the next one now. To answer your questions. The questions that you have that will serve many. (This is such a soft sparkling feminine presence. I realize the others have seemed male or neutral though I didn't particularly notice that. Now I notice the contrast.)

Thank you.

June 8-9, 1999 ~
Shilogh (I see him sitting on his horse, his feet in moccasins, hanging freely.)

We would speak. My horse and I.

Greetings, Shilogh. Ho!

We would speak with sadness about dear Mother Earth and her peoples. Human people forget that animals, insects, rocks, trees, are Mother Earth's peoples also. They would easily forget in order to have what they want, thinking this is right/their right. It has not always been so. Times there have been here when beings revered beings. Now is a time human people have forgotten how to watch out for, even, how what they do affects others. They have forgotten how to ask and instead take what they want and leave what they don't want in unbeautiful neglect. Hard it is for me to see this with eyes that are knowing eyes. Sad it is to be with understanding when this is the understanding. Who will teach our children then, when parents have forgotten? Sad it is to see our Earth Mother in pain and feel it in my being. (He prods his horse with his heels. He hasn't looked at me but has spoken, speaking to a place between his horse's ears. I watch now as they move off. I feel the sadness.)

June 12, 1999 morning, writing room, with tea

Justify

What does it mean to justify? It means to make excuse. For not acting in your brilliance – from who you really are. As you make your actions, as you make your thoughts, consider this: Who am I? Not Who am I to do this? To be saying this? and so limit yourselves, as is your wont. But Who am I ? in the greater sense, the larger sense that knows. Your godself.

Say this, Who am I? And then say, How do I act? Which means to you, Now that I recognize/remember, how do I act from who I know myself to be? And from there, choose your action, choose your thought – which is action's inventor. The action is its own justification when you act from this place and little will you find your time made up of excuses.

June 13-14, 1999 ~

Truly, you are our hope, for through you, many will hear our words. This is not a fickle thing you do, picking up the pen to write. This is courageous, determined action where action is called for. We applaud. Much is accomplished by beings with a will toward action. Beings willing to be directed, accept guidance, for the highest good of themselves and others. Something sparkly happens around this, as you see. We applaud, then, the willingness to keep awake during your sleep time to gather words and messages and record them. Something there is very loving in this. And this love comes through in the writing. Think not that your contribution is small, but honor it as we honor it with our thanks/ gratitude.

We honor the sleep time, as well, and the realms you visit there, and the assistance you offer and provide where it is needed and does make a difference. No, don't be shy about hearing this, for it is true of others who will hear it through your words. And even as we give you the message, they will know it is for them. It will speak to them, and animate them, and congratulate them, as it is meant to.

Remember you are a spokesperson, a messenger for us and shine in our words, as you are meant to. Celebrate that this is so. Feel it true around you. What you give, others receive, as truly, we do also. It is a gift to us, even as it is/seems a gift to you. And a gift for others through you.

Without you, it might not arrive. And in such a pretty package. We have chosen wisely. It is not yours to doubt this. Sleep well for in sleep you are also divine.

Is there anything you would tell the world for their/our enlightenment?

Tell the world, Be patient. What seems as though it will never come is coming closer. Act with love that it may be called and made welcome.

How do we act with love? How do we know how to do this?

You know because you act as if every other person is the beloved. You know because you act as if you, yourself, are the beloved. And indeed, you are. And when you act from knowing this, every situation is something you can smile upon. Be patient. Be lovéd.

How beautiful. Thank you. Good night.

Adieu. Fare thee well. Be lovéd.

Gentle me into the night for I am longing to meet you. Am lusting for the service I find in dreaming. Am alive to possibility and love. Which seems devotion. Gentle me. Here I come. Arms open. Wings lifting.

June 14, 1999 morning

I invoke source, that which dances me and makes me cry from that place where the tears start. (knock) I ask to be an instrument of good will, an instrument of divine instruction.

You are these and more. We know it is not out of insecurity you ask this. We assure you, nonetheless. That what you ask you are already being. An instrument of divine peace on this planet. And this are you being also. Know you not that as you walk, you radiate brilliance. Light. That as you smile, you do this also.

Be not confused by others' reactions to what they see. They are seeing your light. They are telling you what is true. The effect you have on one person may change that person's day and he may remember that day as something special and it may be a beacon in his world and so it may change his life. Or otherwise, does it not happen that in that day he smiles upon someone else? And isn't this really what we call love? And is it not a blessing?

Seek not for glorious overtoppling of things, for what you do is quiet and quietly changing the world. Why not? Is it not your intention? Your devotion to bring peace. Peace smiles around you. Do not doubt it. Look at others – how they show you this quality in you, and know it deep inside you to your very core.

June 16-17, 1999 ~

I'm here if there's anything else to convey. I'm here.

Here. Here under the tree, (I hear a voice and see the tree. The voice seems feminine, playful. Twinkle voice.)

Each of us is to develop a place of light that is our own. That we can return to.

June 20-21, 1999 ~

Shilogh?

Yes. Shilogh is here and brings you greetings. You are learning much in your travels. This is comfortable?

Very. And exciting.

Brood not on what others you love are doing a way you wouldn't do it. They have to find their ways – and means – the same way you are doing. What if they didn't find their own guidance because you could make everything right? You are holding love. This is all that you need to do.

Namaste.

CHAPTER NINE

People forget.
I ask you to remember.

June 21-22, 1999 ~

Any one want to come through?

We are wanting you to know peace and joy and contentment. We are wanting you to know love and strength. We are eager to help you do so. Even as you want these for yourself, we want them for you. (Oh, I see, I think this message for me when actually for the many *and* me.)

Let us help you with this. Feel not you must do it all yourself. Many are we ready to help when you are ready to be helped. Relax into our arms and be lifted by letting go. Letting go constraints and expectations. Letting go pride, which keeps you rigid. Letting go. Letting go. So that what you do and how you do it comes into alignment with Source and we may help you as you ask.

Right it is and gentle that this should happen. For us it does. The worries you keep yourself tied to can dissolve and set you free. Many there are who will hear these words and say, How do I let go? I'm responsible. No. It is that you accept responsibility *with* the guidance coming to you instead of trying to work without it. And so doing, will things flow more easily and be accomplished without strain and without worry. Try this. You can always take back the worries if you don't like to be without.

On liberation. You set your own selves free. Of expectations and methods you have imposed. You and those around you. Notice what those bonds are – bounds. And choose whether to release them. We are here to help.

June 23, 1999 afternoon under the tree

I wish to speak of tragedy and its worth. What is tragedy but things not going your way? Yes. You do not call "tragedy" when you agree with what is happening, but when you disagree. And eager you are to disagree with things that happen without your consent. But who has made a rule that things need your consent? You would not consent to some things that are the best thing for you. Or for others – for you feel you must consent for them (others), too.

You would not consent to hurt your own finger, perhaps, and yet, when you do, it somehow serves you. There is learning in this for you to know. There is enlightenment. Empowerment.

Someone is here on his cushion in orange light. Chinese-type robes. A bun of black hair on the top of the head. About 3 or 4 feet above ground.

"Listen wisely to wisdom which comes in many forms," he leans over the edge of the cushion to tell me. "Especially those you least suspect. Who but a wise one listens to all things for what they have to teach him. And spends no time with sticking labels on."

June 23-24, 1999 ~

Well, I'm here. Ready to be enlightened.

So are we. What are you asking?

Can you tell me about ascension? Do I understand it? Can you put it into words? An explanation for our understanding?

You would like us to enlighten your understanding of ascension. Is it beings being lifted into air? Disappearing into light? Leaving one place for another? From your current point of view it would seem so.

Imagine a fold in fabric. You can be on the outside of one side of the fold and see in one direction or on the other side of the fold and see in the other direction or *on* the fold which brings together both those places. Ascension is the fold.

June 26,1999

You have something you'd like to say?

Yes. You are very wise – to follow guidance instead of self – small self. Small self pulls you this way and that with questions. Did I do this right? Was I supposed to do something else? And no answers. Only answer, maybe.

Guidance answers questions, keeps one steady path through many directions. You are learning this, wise one. This we call surrender. This willingness to be guided.

Like a child you first must know the experience of "no." Must taste it, spit it, throw it around and find out what it does – what reactions it can cause. First must test the limits of this power.

Nothing is lost or wasted in experience. Experience directs. And this is your direction now and now you have a star that's steady and holds firm, always where you look when you look for it.

Show others their star and how to see it and how to find it and how to know it's there. This you do with your work, with your words, and especially with your example.

Many are the children who grow tired of saying no. And want to be fully children and discover every thing else. Show them how to do it. Be not afraid to speak. The ones near you will listen and then ones farther and farther off.

This is service in the highest sense. This is what you're meant for, happiest in, tuned with true direction.

How can we express our joy that this is so? (They lift the hems of what look like togas and all together dance a little jig.)

Your words to you are words to all who will listen and find them in themselves. Be not holding back with them. But share with generosity. As we recognize you, we recognize those who resonate the message for themselves.

Do not keep it secret then, for they who are ready, understand and they who are not will later say, Oh, *that's* what that was about.

Fear not their judgment for they will just dismiss you as being crazy. (They are very amused at this and nodding that I've written it down and pointing and laughing at their wit.)

So always, whatever we give you can be shared with everyone else. Those beings who are ready will find themselves in this and eagerly accept the learnings and pass them on.

And so we are accomplished. And so, also, are you.

Thank you. Anything about the ascension?

The ascension is a natural process, even if unusual. Unusual meaning rare, not common to your experience. Some of you may remember other times you have ascended, but mostly, new experience can tend to block it out.

The techniques you teach can help in clearing bodies, clearing forms, can familiarize beings with a process. All work that is of a clearing nature makes the body lighter, more capable of light.

These are processes which open an understanding beyond understanding. An acceptance beyond having-to-know. Meditation can also help this. And some of the martial arts – which we term "arts for enlightenment." The meditation art, the martial arts, can help beings know their advancement, see their progress – which you so much like to see.

Teach those who come to you to learn. Those who are ready will be there.

And for those who are not close enough? You're writing the books.

This sounds like an advertisement to me.

It is. It is an endorsement. We endorse – from our perspective what you are doing from yours. The teachings are meant to make the ascension more comfortable, less unknown. The teachings are meant to be answerings. That which beings carry in their awareness need not cause them fear or distrust. And experience is a wonderful way to inform awareness.

Awareness of being guided makes awareness of being safe. Don't you feel safe, wise one, in being guided?

Yes. Amazingly so. As well as in having choice.

Yes. Choice. You are not meant to give up choice because you have found direction. As you are finding, when you know your direction, there are many good ways to get there.

We are here and we are helping, not telling you what to do.

Yes. I feel that. Thank you. I can enjoy myself so much more not being frantic about "What should I be doing?"

Ah, yes. You kept yourself *quite* frantic with it. We enjoy that you willingly sit now, outside, under a tree.

Thank you. Is this et al? Yes.

You are welcome. We always welcome you.

June 27, 1999 writing room

You are deeply loved. Doubt not our sincerity in this. Many are the times you might have said, no, I choose to do this instead, and not have written.

But always you choose writing and make it possible for us to bring you words. Are you picturing them in gift baskets? Yes. This is so.

And those gift baskets go out to those who are ready to read these words. And there will be a change. Easy it would be to undervalue these words and this writing. Easy because of the profound change they will cause. Much of the world is not ready. But many there are who are eager. Yes, thirsty, to learn this. To have this sustain their faith, nurture their yearning, and prepare them a way.

"Home is where the heart is" and the heart is always home. Many are the distresses caused in the world because the hearts know this and are being silenced. Much is the courage that is needed to open to hearing the heart. The heart tells you things you don't want to know, don't want to surrender to.

And yet, the heart knows, remembers, what you came here for. The heart knows what you don't remember and will tell you if you listen. When you are not in alignment with what your heart knows, it will disturb your quiet, disrupt your body, unsettle your mind so you'll listen.

You will know what your heart knows if that is your greatest good. And here is how to listen so it need not disrupt your sleep.

A meditation:

Find yourself a quiet place. Outside under trees is best. Or if not that, then anywhere that you find comfortable. And imagine yourself. It's summertime. You are outside on a warm enough day with just a gentle breeze. Birds are making small bird sounds, not enough to disturb you. Trees are lifting their branches and letting their leaves twinkle and you might even see their lights – like fireflies in the dusk on a twilight evening in June.

You've found a comfortable place to sit down and are letting your seating hold you, like hands that are holding you safe.

You remember being this loved, this taken care of. And here you are again in this wonderful leaning-back-into, this comfortable letting-go.

Perhaps your eyes are closed and you remember when that was, or maybe you imagine when that might have been.

And you ask your body now to release its hold just a little and you draw in light into all your spaces. Picture this however feels right to you. An image will come and it will be just the right one for you at this time.

And as the spaces in you fill with light, you feel yourself expand with lightness. And maybe you start to feel fuzzy at the edges and maybe you don't. And maybe you feel a little tingly in your hands or feet and maybe you don't.

And from here we can see you, full of light and lifting a little, just slightly off the ground, and so we can know you are ready to ask your heart. And so you phrase the question and prepare to hear the answer. The answer from your heart may come to you as a feeling, a word, a group of words. It may come to you as a picture. You must pay attention to what comes first, as soon as you ask the question, before you try to interpret or doubt or question and so get in your own way.

Later you may do all those things if you choose. For now you need to be still and accept as a gift what the heart brings to you.

So now if you're ready, in the stillness and the quiet, and without expectations or limitations, we ask the heart, respectfully, "What is it you'd like me to know?"

Listen. Appreciate. Accept the gift and give thanks.

You may look at the gift and touch it and admire it in the place you are in now. But let not your fingerings turn it into something else lest you lose it bringing it back.

Stay there as long as you like and when you're ready, thank your heart for the message and for guiding you in this life and, again, become aware of the trees. And the twinkles underneath the leaves. And breathe a bit more deeply now and feel the hands gently holding you, and then the chair or seating. Settle comfortably into your body and feel the light in all your spaces.

And when you are ready, open your eyes. And notice that even in the fully-present, your heart's gift still has substance, meaning, value. Something to tell you.

And so over the next few hours or days that gift may take different forms, but, no matter how much you play and change it to understand what it is, always you can come back to it exactly as it was given, in its perfect shape and meaning as given you from the heart.

And know you can return at any time and ask your heart again. And your heart will tell you what you most need to know and guide you.

June 28-29, 1999 ~
Shilogh

Good it is and wise that you respond to someone's needing. It is not easy to hold your own space and someone else's though sometimes necessary. You are learning to hold your own space and let others respond to you. This is a strong place to be, a place of strength.

You are building and shaping your mountain for others to come to you. Angelic beings notice this and are here to help you. We like the idea of Pine Grove (workshops at Spiritualist summer camp). Much to be learned and share. Be careful, though, to put your own impressions first. Test others' impressions against them. This is as it should be. Others can show you some things to look at which, then, you will examine. Tender are the feelings for this. You can always honor the feelings. Others' impressions bring clarity and also mystery. Limit not with the small impressions. Instead, expand the large.

Many are the good things in store for you. As you ask for them, they come. Tea is a part of your diet. Good for many uses. Don't give it too much importance. It works for you.

Relax now. Tomorrow's trip is taken care of. Already complete. You will see the change you make. And so will others. This is an angel-of-mercy trip. Revel in your role. All is well.

Thank you. (I see him now at the edge of the forest. In feathered bonnet and buckskin? Shirt and leggings. It must be warm in those, I suggest. Too warm, and he's dressed simply in breech clout and moccasins. He holds a staff with 2 feathers tied at the top. I don't see his horse and then I do as she moves forward.)

Thank you both for coming.

You're welcome. It's our pleasure. (They fade backwards and the woods are quiet.)

June 29-30, 1999

All is well with us and with you. And how was your trip? (We did some guided self-healing and she cleared an issue that had been bothering her.)

Even as you said. It was delightful. What a wise child this is. Where did she come from?

The Pleiades and beyond. She is needed here now and so she chose this service. What she clears and balances for herself, she clears and balances for others. The world – I do not exaggerate – will feel a shift as she clears her field. It is not too much to say she is doing work with the issue she chose today to cause a path for others to heal.

Brave being. She confronts herself. As she resolves what she has begun, she creates the template. You understand? For others to be able to do this – not hold on and hurt and cause hurt and resonate hurt but release and make space for light. This is what is changing on the planet now. The negativity must leave and so is playing out in different forms. Brave being, she is standing firm in acknowledgement of self. Without judgment, with intent upon good. And as she does, she sets in place the possibility of this healing on the planet. It is no small thing.

Not that this has never been done – but that she sets a way clear to do it with love and honor herself in the doing. For this are the lightworkers here.

She is finding her importance is she not?

I think she'll be happy to resolve for herself. That's what she's looking for now.

Then you must tell her. We would have her know. She feels she doesn't accomplish much and yet, she holds the light. She will discover this on her own, but you may tell her now. And as she clears this negativity, she will see it transformed to help her forward motion.

I feel as if I'm thinking this next part.

You are thinking it, yes, but we are telling you also. Why don't you listen and let her see for herself if it resonates with what she knows?

She will feel a readiness to act on her knowing. (Oh. This is different from what I was thinking.) And why you listen instead of think just now.

She will feel a readiness to have this event behind her. When the heart expands, it constricts/is constricting to keep it small.

She will know how to act. She cannot do it wrong. She has gone past blaming herself and will speak from a new place she's found.

Even though she may remember it, the old pattern has dissolved. She is a shining being and will find that in herself.

All is well. Sleep tight. Adieu.

June 29-30, 1999 ~
For someone

Truly you are being re-aligned in more ways than one. Revel in this being so. What you have wanted is coming. Relax now. Tip not so far forward in your excitement that you cause the forward and back wobble that needs readjustment. Keep your head in adjustment over your feet/ in a straight line above them – that maintains balance. You know this is for your growth, wise one. What are you learning?

June 30-July 1, 1999 ~

I ask St. Germaine of the violet flame to help with an issue. Each of us puts her/his ego into the metal bowl I see, and instantly there is a flash of light as they're purified, made pure. The flash goes out sideways instead of up, as if something above presses down on the bowl.

Good morning. I'm here if anyone wants to come. (I see circle of my starry family. I'm awake. I hear the crow.)

The crows are bringers of stories. They have an important job to wake you so you don't sleep through them (the stories). Crow is a ferocious pest to sleep. He hangs stories all round and in full morning, leaves. Watch and listen for crow, for around him you find stories. (I'm aware of a light touch on my upper lip. Open my eyes and look out to see water. Trees as seen from above. With water beyond.)

July 1, 1999

People forget. I ask you to remember.

Shilogh wishes to greet you. And say you are taking the role of the warrior. Congratulations. Nor is it easy to step into a place where someone may sling you arrows. And yet, you have your shield and you are bold and you allow us to protect you. Sing your warrior song and dance your warrior dance for this are you, also.

We see you and be glad for your coming into your power. For knowing when not to hold back what is yours to give and for knowing when it is yours to demand what is right for you to take. Gentle you are in this and strong and stand so in your power. Watch and see the change that will be as you reveal your self – the self that is working with god within you and allowing it to shine forth. How can it not be beautiful to see you so. (I'm crying.)

Channel for others, yes.

But ask for yourself, also. And take what we offer. Why hide the best in you when you don't hide anything else?

This book is going fine. No. You shouldn't be working harder. You have found the key. Relax. Let all things come to you. Let us provide for your wants and your comfort. And for your book. This needs not to be hectic but to be calm. And so it is quite appropriate to have your needs met in all fields.

You may wear my costume if you like as you take on your warrior self. If it makes it fun. It is yours.

> He's taking off his shirt and putting it around me. Now the beads. The feathered headdress. "I think I'll keep the leggings," he says. "The shirt is long enough on you. Now stand like this," he says, and gives me his spear to hold, anchored to the ground.
>
> He stands with his head up, proud and solemn and gazing into the distance. "See where you are going," he says, "as if you have already been there, many times, and here you come again, knowing how to do this, knowing all is well."
>
> He stands beside me and we look. I smell the grass, the trees. I feel the feathers move in a small breeze. I am part of the earth and part of the sky, and he nods as I notice this. And in all directions my intent goes out. In front of me, behind me, to the left of me, to the right, above me, below me.

I stand in my power and the universe takes notice. I feel he has stepped away to let me stand alone and know that the power is my power, not something that leans on him. And I feel him step back so I will know I don't have to stand alone.

I am memorizing all of this, especially how I stand.

"Use your voice," he says.

And I say, "Ho!" And my voice goes out and echoes back to me.

"Your voice carries your power," he says. "Don't forget to use it."

And we stand and the breeze ruffles the feathers, and I know that I am loved.

I breathe in. I breathe out. And find myself, also, sitting here.

Ho! And thank you for my lesson.
And this is true speech. Yes.
Shall we come back and get started? (on book)

Yes. When you're ready. Gently. And full of love. (From here I see me standing, still holding my place. With him, my teacher and my guide.)

July 2, 1999 deep meditation, writing room, morning

Am I back? Anything I'm supposed to know from there?

You're supposed to know you are loved. Do you know it yet? We will keep telling you.

CHAPTER TEN

Take heart. Honor yourself.

July 2, 8, 1999

Warrior stands in her power
Stands in her grace
as do you.
Warrior lifts up her voice
and lets herself be known.
Warrior lets herself dance.
Warrior stamps her feet
and shakes her rattle
and wakens the gods.
Time is it now for warrior
to stand in her own knowing,
speak in her own truth.
As the bear marks the tree
with its claws,
warrior makes her mark on the world.
Let her people remember
what she is here for.
Let her people awake
as warrior remembers.
Let her spread the peace
she has come to bring
and light the skies with her being.

Ho. It is well remembered.

July 2-3, 1999 ~

We've been waiting.

Thank you.

Are you alert?

I think so. (They make motions to each other as I've slept pretty soundly all night and it's morning.)

We would tell you something.

Yes, please.

For your book.

Yes.

It is progressing lovely. Don't begin to fret. You do well without it (fretting). Disengage from thoughts of publishing. This will be arranged. You will know what to do.

The ascension?

The ascension is already happening. You think of it as a whoosh. Not so. Already you are changing things in your bodies, in your thought fields. Already change is happening. Don't you notice? You give something a term, a name, and then give it expectations.

Instead, you could watch it unfold and experience it. And so know what it is.

You don't want to be taken by surprise? And must needs know ahead. But every small change you are making changes the overall change. You see how this is so.

Awareness is necessary. And awareness causes awareness. So, how will it be? It will be as you have learned, a shift to another dimension, gentle or dramatic. It may be as you experienced in a dream, a physical lifting into light or a lifting through, breaking through into clear air above a place that seems like home.

Is that why I had more than one experience in the same dream?

To show there is no one way for everyone. Yes. In the dream you were with two different people – two different ways for the same thing happening.

And this was the ascension?

Yes. Experienced the ways they chose. And you were with them to see it, to be able to tell it here.

Ah. I liked them both. They both were beautiful.

And you preferred the "going home." To a place you love on earth.

Yes. Does this mean I'll come back to teach because I love it?

It is likely so.

And others choose that also?

Others choose their own paths after their own ascension. Some will come back to earth to serve, but in ascended state. Others will go where their hearts will call them. Very much as it would be here, if you would allow yourselves to follow your heart's calling.

We speak of after ascension because you use it to mean a certain Event. But understand, you have already begun. As you choose, already it is occurring. It may not be a flash of light, but these gentle things you are doing, that change all else that is and put you in the different state. Act deliberately, then, from what you know is love. Accept that you are aligning. Accept that your call is heard.

We are joyous at the amount of change that you all/collective are occurring.

We see your light. We see your intent. We see the shifts you create. The shifts in consciousness, in clarity, in energy. As you clear negativity, you create space for light. As you send light into spaces where light has not been, you expand the spaces. Imagine how beautiful it is for us to see this.

And as you do this, create this, expand this, your bodies respond. And what is the ascension process except turning your bodies to light. Think not little of what you are doing, then. But think much.

But think in lightness. What your bodies show of light can be seen by others or felt by others. You give them, then, the possibility of what they can be. And aren't you already teaching, then? And hasn't ascension already begun?

Don't wait for the horns and the trumpets. Be in ascension now. As you already are.

Thank you.

There's more. When you think you're trying to get somewhere, you forget to notice.

Notice everything. Don't wait until you're there. Notice things around you now and appreciate them.

July 3-4, 1999 ~
Shilogh

Be wary of making attachments that then link you with things. Be wary of having your strength drawn away by things you do not approve. As you live in your day, make your choices of where and what will serve you and where and what to serve. You are flowing nicely and so now look for the small things that can impede your flow.

Look to set them out of your path and so flow easily past them. Don't make rocks and set them in your stream. Set any rocks up on the banks and flow by.

July 5-6, 1999 ~

Is there a message?

Death is no more. What you are experiencing on the planet is the change from death. You are clearing now what needs to be cleared for this change. What you have feared is not coming. As you truly embrace the christ consciousness, a change takes place. A restructuring that has consequences.

Instead of death is a coming into light/life. This is no small thing for yourselves and your planet.

Think not of the ways things used to be but instead of how they are becoming. As you unlimit yourselves and release your held beliefs, so you release the patternings of what has been and allow what might be. And what might be is a gradual/gentle lifting in vibration. What might be is a coming home to light without the transition you know as death. A coming home to light with full awareness and intent.

What are we doing here now but changing the vibration that this be so.

You who are here and who experience the thinning of the veil between worlds are able to tell me this is so. Are able to feel the change in everything around you and in you, your own selves. Is it not so?

July 7, 1999, morning chant

> I chant, lift my arms, rounded, shoulders down, feel the energy gather. See in front of me to my left, Jesus, to the right, Mary and Kwan Yin. Then the bear in the center. Shilogh? Sense and see him behind me to my right. I beam the energy to them. They stand like a cast on stage at the end of a play.
>
> Faeries come in from the right, followed by the elves. They cross between the stage and where I stand.
>
> Mary looks at the others. Slides the fabric off her head, steps to where I'm standing, to my right, and merges partway into me. The cast nod and smile their approval. Shilogh stamps the end of his spear on the ground. The cast applaud. Energy beams off me. I feel lifted a little, from the ground, can see my feet relax, not holding me up, as I am held up in the energy.
>
> We stand, our heads uncovered, Mary and I, and my embrace, arms lifted, includes her.
>
> I am slightly above her. See her pull the cover up over her head and bow her head. No, no, I shake my head. It feels as though she is my child.

Uncovered, like this. I lift my chin. I feel rays spray out around my head. And she lets the cloak down and steps into me. I feel her head at my breastbone where she is looking out. I am her cloak, her protector.

I am now aware of the cast again, who watch as if we are on stage. And I/we grow larger and larger and higher and stream out in light and stars.

Faeries fly off in all the directions that the light is going.

The characters on stage seem small now, and very far away.

And Shilogh, also, is looking up to see us lifting further.

I feel a sense in my third eye.

It seems there may be angels up here, but I haven't seen any. It is very open feeling. Like at the beach but also without any land. Now I am being wrapped in cords of light in all directions. Not close to what feels like my body, but farther out. I see these with the image of how we used to wrap a balloon with string and when the balloon went down, the delicate wrapping would still be intact.

And this is what they're doing. While I'm this big. Wrapping me in light that will stay this shape and size around me when I've gone back. They tuck in the end – these beings I cannot see but know are there and what they're doing.

Mary reaches her arms wide out of my chest and she is smiling. She is comfortable now and happy. She is being taken care of. The spirals of light around us glow. The beings are finished and stand back. And, almost, I can see them. Made of light, standing, oh, the way auras might look without the people in them.

I think it's time we go back. I think they're letting us go.

Mary has folded her hands to her chest inside my chest.

We can expand and the cords of light expand with us. We can come back and the surround of light comes with us to fit our size. And I'm understanding now, that it will come with us in appropriate size when we go back to the stage on earth or wherever we were when we started this. The light will stay expanded around but in appropriate size to our size. This is so Mary can feel safe and I can feel safe with her.

I'm drifting now, through scenes around here, and come back to the place where Shilogh stands, holding the place for me. And as I arrive, Mary steps out and bows Namaste to me. And I bow Namaste. She steps back on stage. The cast clasp hands and bow.

The faeries fly through from left to right and the elves dance along behind them. They seem to be drawing an airy curtain. Shilogh stamps the end of his spear on the ground. The cast fades slowly backwards.

I feel Mary's arms reach out of my chest. I see them there. I can see the spirals of light that surround me, my gift from the gods. And now I see white roses and, in front of me, green lawn. I am full of energy sparkles.

I seat myself to sing and to drum on the earth with my hands. Goosebumps big time as I anchor this experience in mother earth. And the faeries come and the elves are dancing as I sing. Behind me, Shilogh sits also. I see, in the distance, the bear twirl and dance.

And so, with Shilogh singing now and drumming the earth, with bear dancing, with the faeries and elves spraying light, I come back here.

July 8, 1999
For someone

You think you must make a quick decision, but you must not. Notice how your daughter pauses before she answers a question? This is a great gift. One she is teaching you.

Pause and listen. If you're not sure, you can say, "Please give me a moment on that." And if you're still unsure, say, "I'm unsure about that." Take your time to decide and be comfortable with your decision. Otherwise your no's become yes's. You see the pattern this sets up.

You are guiding by steering way to the left, back-paddling, way to the right. Instead, see clearly where you want to arrive and go there. Don't push the canoe off-shore until you see where you're going. Then, when your children see where to go, they will paddle easily and well with no amount of wasted effort. You all will arrive with comfort and ease.

You know how to do this. You get caught in quick response. Don't do that. Explain this change to your children. When you respect their boundaries this way, you'll find that they respect yours. They will learn to respect each other's.

Each of you needs private space/time to not be interrupted. As you honor this and listen to what you really want and convey it lovingly, their needs are met and so are yours.

Children will not be put on a shelf, but will keep demanding their needs be met. You see this. Become a child yourself. Demand your needs be met in such a way that they learn the appropriate way to do this. With respect of others and yourself.

No arbitrary answers. You know the answers. Give yourself time to access them and honor them enough to pursue them.

This is worldly advice in a worldly matter. See if it resonates with you. Test it in your heart – your heart full of love and goodness and delight. When you speak out from this heart, all other hearts respond.

Be and your children will be with you. Be loving. Be not arbitrary. Be not changing what you say. They will fit easily into this comfort level you create.

Your husband will also feel the change. As you allow yourself to be the person you already are without imposing restrictions on yourself.

Thank you. This is all for now. Be you (Randeane) a guide for this if an example is needed. Explain if it needs explaining. Thank you.

Don't let your first word be no and your second word be yes. This is confusing. And becomes a pattern. Choose the pattern you want, not the one you received.

July 9, 1999 8 a.m., writing room, chant, arm movements

Any messages? For whom? For someone

Take heart. Your project prospers. Truly, are you meant to change the world. The world is ready to hear what you say. And know you that any change causes a shift in world consciousness. Your book is a book of love (goosebumps). Treat it with respect for it comes from a place of love (goosebumps). Treat it with honor. And honor yourself for the writing of it (goosebumps). For the heart connection you feel with the intention. This is more than romance. This is love. The long-lasting stuff this world can produce only with commitment. Honor yourself for that commitment. It is no small thing.

Whatever needs doing next, do. The time is ready now for the world to explore this something-not-shallow. Don't you see that why you wrote it is this? Stop stalling and go forward. Delight in the doing of any part of bringing this book to people who will learn. Who will smile (goosebumps) and say, Yes. This is possible in our time, in our world today. You have made for them a template, a new way of seeing, and this is not a small thing. This is a grand thing and we honor you for your doing this with integrity and sincerity and good intent. We see your bright heart shining. In this book you put it forth (goosebumps).

Be not held back by little doubts and questionings – oh – or big doubts and questionings. Instead put one foot in front of the other and you have taken the next step. Continue in this manner and you are there. Delight now in your accomplishment – for accomplishment it is. It is appropriate and necessary that you congratulate yourself. As we do. All is well.

Meager are the rewards at this time and so you must stay eager. Though you do not see where you're going, still you must stay going with purpose and intent.

You do not sit down for other projects. Do not sit down for this. But carry it forward as you do the others and see it achieved.

This being, Randeane, is here to encourage you. Ask for encouragement. She is proud of you in all ways and knows how to honor this part of you that you seldom allow to be seen. Renew yourself with things you enjoy. Take good care of yourself. And ask that others take care of you, too. For you are worthy and deserving of attention – from yourself and others. The attention that makes you feel comfortable – not that which makes you feel foolish.

Some of the energy you spend on others can now be spent on yourself. If not now, when?

Look inside daily and notice your acts of love and know that what you have written can float – you have caused the buoyancy by repeating, truly, what is in your heart.

The good this book can cause with those who are ready to hear, can shift a planet. Do not doubt it, but believe it and so draw it to you.

We are sincere in this. The consciousness of one person changing affects the consciousness of the collective and one person makes a difference. We applaud your generosity of spirit in doing this work. And we advise you to play. You will find you have created space for it.

And for light. Throw your hood back and feel the light. And breathe.

We love you. We honor and respect you. Heed your own yearnings for they lead you there.

Adieu. Goodspeed. Fare Well.

Think not we jest. We would not waste your time. All is well. Expand.

(I do an invocation. I invite ascended masters to sit in circle around me. Jesus comes in behind me. Then I see him in front of me, to my left, hands together, head bowed to them.)

The work you do is wholesome, needed, secure. Not tentative, but firm. It will hold. Be assured.

Thank you.

We are delighted to have you with us again. Sitting in our circle. In your rightful place. It has been many years. (As he says this, I notice I am sitting in a circle with others.)

Take now the time to acclimate. And be at ease.

You sit in the company of strangers who are not strangers at all. You will see. Be comfortable. We invite you. You did not just stumble in here. You have come at our request. That you know this as home to you, also, and feel not so estranged.

Dire is it, indeed, when you feel estranged from your home. And so it is right that you understand to be as one who lives here – who can open the refrigerator if she wants.

> He looks to see if I've appreciated this. I have. We both are smiling now. I am more comfortable. He shows his hand around the circle for me to look at the others. I do. I think it's Dunna there, across from me, rather laughing that I've found him. There seems a penant? or banner with gold fringe, like the head of a Chinese dragon ahead and to my right. There is a throne there also with no one seated on it. No one is talking or moving around. It seems fine for me to sit still and close my eyes.
>
> Now as if from standing behind me, I see the spiral wrappings of light around me and tall above. I drift. See violet light in the center as if instead of a campfire. Now on the wall in front of me here, with my eyes closed, I read: Jesus Christ (with under it, my phone number) and now the face of the bear fills the screen and the bear says:

I am talking to *you.*

Okay. I'm listening.

> Do not put your head on backwards to see where you have been. Follow where your nose points forward. Watch for the claw marks I put on trees for you to follow. I guided you here.

Thank you.

> Get your own rest and your own play so that you stay open. These things will also get typed so don't close down hard on that. (He shows his paws.) But not by me. (Shakes his head. I'm laughing.)
> There are those who help you get out of your own way and so the typing goes faster and can be enjoyed.

This running around isn't needed but it does you good. It keeps you light and happy and aware.
I am finished speaking.

Thank you, bear.

I live here, too, he says, and rolls on the floor beyond where the others are sitting.

Does this place have a name?

It has been called Nirvana. (Jesus answering.) We know you will go back now. Come again when you will. We miss you when you're gone and applaud what you are doing.

Thank you.

> They pat their hands on the floor beside them. I think as a way of closure, good-bye. Or perhaps they're drumming me here.
> I bow Namaste to Jesus who has remained standing, is beside me now as I come back to a room above stairs with windows.
> He touches the top of my head with his right hand. Puts a finger to his lips.
> "SShh. Waken gently, dear one."
> For a moment I can't tell if he has gone, and then I sense he has, but I still feel his presence clearly. Ah. I see he stands now, a little way off, beaming with his hands. Gently, I come back. Open my eyes. 10:00.

July 10, 1999 chant

Any message? For whom? For someone

Be not discouraged. Take hope. Your health is in good care. Worry not needlessly, but attend to what is wanting. As you structure your day, re-structure your days. That the pattern you set up lead to fullness and joy. Set up your thinking to notice the good in things around you. And do you reflect that good to others. You have a mission here. And your mission is to show love. You have chosen to show love through what looks to be defeating circumstances. Play along, but do not be caught in the illusion you have contrived for your own learning. And when you decide not to play along, change your self in a minute.

Keep not thoughts of love in your heart or love will come back to you.
Keep not thoughts of abundance or abundance will come back to you.
Keep not thoughts of forgiveness or forgiveness will come back to you.
Keep not thoughts of comfort or comfort will come back to you and you will not be playing your part.
Keep not joy in your heart lest you soar above the circumstances you bind around you.
How can you teach if you show the way to live in fulfillment?
No, then, stay rigid and hold firm the beliefs that limit you.
So to pull the love from our hearts. So to pull the understanding. Who would understand if you walked in freedom and greatness? Who would learn from that?
Better you play what you came to play.
But did you intend to stay there? Or did you intend to learn?

Thank you.

Adieu. Fare thee well. Amen.

(I come to the circle of light beings and sit in council, meditation.)

Purely are you led. Purely are you guided. The energies which serve you are of the highest order. Doubt not our dedication to you and your work. Clear is the channel amongst us. (Jesus, Mary, Kwan Yin, bear. Now I seem to be standing.)

All true knowledge begins at home. This is where you find it. "Ask and you shall receive. Knock and it shall be opened."

I'm having trouble understanding this ascension. Is it physical as well as soul progression? What in the physical happens?

In the physical you are filled with light. You transcend time and space. You take your place with the masters.

That sounds like what I'm doing now.

That is what you're doing now.

Then what, please, is the difference? Is there a difference?

Yes. The difference is your body will not be *there* to go back to as a manifestation of your self.

Will my body be there with you? Yes.

And how will my body get there?

By being more and more filled with light.

It will just float up?

Yes. In a manner of speaking. When your body reaches a certain lightness you will find it here. Better to say, though, when you reach a certain lightness. You think "body" because you are there and have it to go back to. Here you will think of "I" and not of body.

Is this something I need to understand?

You don't need to understand it. A term defines something – which means it narrows it down and this cannot be defined. Let go of your perceptions of "understand" and know you are becoming lighter. Know that your shining intent carries forth your purpose.

Come here as often as you like and the term for it will not matter. (They are nodding and smiling that this is true. That this is something they know.)

I am the Christed One. I come in many forms to be among you. And always you try to define me, instead of learn what I teach. Find the Christ energy within you and then you will know me and *my* prayers be answered. A person needs come home.

July 11, 1999 writing room, morning chant

Thank you. (I see my voice go up, clearing the hollow flute.)

Any messages?

You make plans with Spirit. This is good. You include each other in your plans. It is easy to keep separate – your own thoughts going one direction or in circles without connecting to the greater good.

It is easy because of how you are trained for here. So much you must learn. And then forget. You become so filled with what you learn that you don't remember you are not separate and you don't listen to that which can teach you you're not. You have made pathways comfortable to go around and around again and do not step onto the fresh snow out of your fox and geese. Learn to step out. Use all the snow. It is here for you. Make new designs and new designs and, Yes, of course, snow angels. Use up all the snow in this sparkling sunlight because there is more and more.

It is in the snow beyond the game that spirit whispers and dances and shouts. And the edges of snow have no edges but meet in the middle – which is no middle as you know it here and yet you understand it.

The fox and geese game is for you to notice and step outside into vastness that is you. Into space that keeps on going and is not confined. Beyond the male + and the female O is something more. And you are invited into that something more.

At first see your footsteps in the snow. Before they go into the sky.

Revel. All is well-arranged for your being. We rejoice at your play which invites us to play as well.

Oh, boy. Here she is, dancing out again. Into our field of snow. Where we can dance and hear her song and add our own.

Anything else? I've asked about the ascension I'm curious about. Anything you'd like to tell me or others through me? I'd like to learn what you have to teach.

You are learning well, child. You are learning well.

Significant, we find it, that you sit and still the world so you may listen. Significant and flattering, needed, thrilling. Time is precious on your earth, and you spend your precious coins to do this. We appreciate.

It is my pleasure, truly, to hear your words.

Rest now. We'll see what it is we wish to say.

Who is here to connect me? (I ask as I feel a presence.)

> I feel someone behind me to my right pulling cords out of where my neck connects to my shoulder and sending them skyward to be plugged in. "It is I," someone says, but I don't see who.
> It is a being of the highest order, connecting me to light. In front of me, I see a circle with wings.
> I'm to receive this light and later I'll know what to do with it, how to use it.
> I sing: *Gladly for aye, we adore thee* (which the church bells are chiming just now).
> Ah. I am seated in the circle. This time there is a child on the throne, lying down, kicking, waving his arms, cooing.
> The company are delighted and smiling and watching. And I am smiling, too. How lovely. I sing again, for the child: *Gladly for aye we adore thee.*
> I am still receiving light and now, seated in the circle, I see the light go out in both directions to the circle around me. And this is possible – that it crosses and keeps going in both directions circling through us, weaving a wreath of light beams. I see me glide back to earth still connected to these light beams that are the same cords I first noticed, but now of light.
> It is beautiful to be here and be part of the wreath.
> (Goosebumps.)

She got it.

Did they really say that?

Yes. (I'm laughing, and the laughing brings me here. Delightedly, opening my eyes. And once more I sing, bringing it here: *Gladly for aye we adore thee.*)

Thank you.

CHAPTER ELEVEN

Your light is your name.

July 12, 1999 morning, writing room, chant

Any messages? For whom? For someone

May you walk in brightness on the earth. May your needs be met in ways you can accept them. Push not away what comes to you for your highest good; and yet, discriminate. Accept not into your field that which unbalances your field. For it is, with you, a delicate balance and the lower vibrations affect it.

Eat foods which support your high vibration. Test if they're good for you. In this way you are feeding your energy rather than depleting it. Drink water which your body needs to sustain the high vibration. You are grounded without the denser energies. It is not that you need to feed them to stay grounded, but that you release them so the energy can ground itself.

As you admit the brilliance of your being, you will see this happen automatically, this adjustment, emotional and physical, to allow the energy spiritual. For now, though, make the way clear to see this by starting with clearing your field.

Express your willingness that this be so and you will be helped. You are not alone. Rather than close down when you know this, open. And be transformed in your knowing. You are learning ways to do this, but sometimes return to habit because habit is familiar and feels safe. Comfort does not mean safety if the body is ill at ease. You may be comfortable in the habit, but the habit brings discomfort of the body. You see?

All vibration is motion and will not be held still. Do not, then, hold yourself still in old patterns that no longer serve you. Put yourself in motion, in vibration, and call the balancing energies. In balance is your safety. In balance is your comfort. What are you holding that no longer serves?

Take off the mask for a moment and acknowledge.

You are a shining light and yet you choose to walk in darkness. You have taught yourself this now. Time for something new. We support you. Others support you. You are safe here.

Look not to lessons of the past now that you have learned them. Hold them not in fear around you as a cloak.

But open the cloak, let it slide off your shoulders and fall to the ground behind you. And look who you be today. And look again tomorrow. For each day are you who you are new in the image of your making.

Limit not yourself with what you have been – or with what you are becoming.

This message comes to you and many can learn from it. Is it not true? There are others you would teach – in the sweet, gentle way you have of loving, heart and soul.

I love you. You are deeply loved. And deeply appreciated for what you bring and what you give freely. We would not see you sad. Or lonely. When, within you is the choice to be loved.

Right food

Right motion

Right thought

Will further the love you bring and share with those around you. Others accept you and love you. Would that you accept and love yourself.

You are a powerful being emanating light to universes. Set aside for just a moment any limitations on how you see you; see how you are. And choose, always choose, how you act.

All is well. Adieu. (I am being kissed on the third eye.)

July 7, 1999

These words are not just for this time and this place. Write them down so they reach others and fulfill their purpose in being spoken. Write them down closely, carefully, each word intact/exact. There is power in words. These words especially. They must be recorded wisely to maintain their power.

July 12-13, 1999 ~

Fifth dimension reality consciousness. This is what we're talking about. This is the teaching in this new age/new time. All over the world are there points of this new consciousness being created by those who are aware. No longer a part of the future. This is part of the present. Now. Worlds within worlds. Energy becoming energy.

Everything you see and own (take responsibility for) will become easier, lighter, full of love. Look for this and notice it happens. You are causing change. You are bringing in the energy that is available now that this be so.

Children, who experience this without comment, without judgment, are doing what children do to bring this energy. The wee ones are not trying to understand what is theirs to accept freely and make their own. They are experiencing, playing, noticing. And so grounding vast amounts of energy. Be you as children in acceptance of what is so. Rather than knock it aside with your beliefs, set aside your beliefs. Already you feel the shift, the change of energies. Make you room/space for this in you that you be blessed and pass this blessing to others.

At the end of this restructuring/centering, you will feel very different, indeed.

July 13, 1999 chanting

Any messages? For someone

Be comforted in your doing. For what you do is right for yourself and others. Make not yourself frantic, but ask assistance from your angels, your guides. They are waiting to assist you. Put down large burdens and request their help and pick them back up lightly.

You cause the heaviness yourself by granting much importance. It is not necessary. Everything you do can be done lightly and with ease. Do not bear down and the weight cannot hold. You empower it with your thoughts.

Step aside and you will see the lightness in all things. We suggest meditation – especially when you don't have time. Re-connect with who you are and you will see clearly how this is so. React not to situations, but choose how you will act. In choosing do you empower lightness and well-being.

What has passed is in the past and you need not call it to you. Let it go. Let it be forgotten. Release it from your body. Give permission that this be so. Your body is made to protect you and keeps protecting you against something even if it no longer needs to. Until your body knows. Inform your body, This is no longer needed. Express your gratitude for being protected.

Inform your body what you need now. And let your body respond to the new program. This is good and very good. Make peace with your body. Make appreciation. All energy serves a purpose. You can change that purpose.

But not with scolding, disapproval. Change with love and acceptance and approval. Your body tells you things. Are you listening? From your body you learn. Become informed. Choose your action and request our help. We are here to serve you. Be at peace.

Thank you very much.

Adieu.

She will understand this?

Or you help to explain it.

> Maybe I am staying here today or maybe I am going into the highest dimensions and bringing back light and anchoring it in the planet. Streams of light as of a waterfall that breaks around the rocks, sends smaller streams in a wider area. I see the light

come and separate and find its destination and draw its own piece of the waterfall/light fall streaming behind it.

And this is how it is now. Light from the highest heavens streaming to thirsty Mother Earth and raising her water table/light table so all who are thirsty may drink and be filled with light.

Think not that this light is for others. Truly, it is for you. A gift to the planet and her peoples from Mother/Father God. All earth's people are thirsty for divine light and all are welcome to drink. And all are welcome home.

Stay discerning. And speak with your heart and so come into center and into balance and into awareness. The energy is coming here and will be spoken. Align you yourself with the highest good and keep true to your purpose. In all of this you thrive.

Be aware in your daily life and meditation what things change and how these things are changing. Watch for the ways to embrace yourself with new love and understanding.

Now are we complete. Now as we see the new lightness glowing in your world.

Thank you.

July 14, 1999 writing room, chant, invoke

Are there any messages today?

What are you wanting?

A message in good spirit for those who will read it.

Sleep you now soundly? Awaken. Open your new eyes to a new world. What has been going on without you? Where has the old world gone? You might notice changes. Vibrancy. Flutters of light at the edges of things as the edges of things soften.

You might notice sparkles of light where they haven't been. You may notice a small high glittering of faery dust as the faeries come forth to do their part to change the world.

Are you still asleep? Have you not noticed a lightness in the air? A gathering of energy in certain places?

Have you not experienced a willingness to speak out? A yearning for all things good, an eagerness to get there?

Why do you hug the pillow and bury your face inside it? The day is calling you. The light is calling you. Come add what you can add. What only you can add to the wisdom and grace of this planet at this time.

Wake into your knowledge of higher self and your own becoming. Wake into the light of Source. Align your heart with the heart of god. For truly, as your heart beats, it sends the call to be aligned. Recognize in you the heartbeat of universes.

Are you sleeping still? Release the things of your past which lull you into slumber, which bid you close your eyes.

Awaken now to all that you are missing. Awaken now to all that is going by.

Let your seeing eyes tell you. Let your hearing ears hear. Allow yourself to be aware.

You are a child. Notice everything anew. Not saying first, "This is this," and then seeing it through that. But saying, "What is this?" and allowing it to inform you. For what the world will tell you today is different from yesterday and the day before though you try to keep it so.

It has already gone past. Wake up and with us make the world that is becoming. And don't stop you there when it has become what it can become today. There is more. Continue to create. The energy is here for your own making. Use it to good intent. For yourself and others.

Celebrate. This is so.

And in your dreams, stay alert. And in your sleep, be aware.

Are you sleeping? Look what has happened without you. See what you can add for harmony and balance, for beauty and peace, for the manifestation of highest good, and waken and add it.

For this will you be praised, will you be honored and adored. That rather than sleep, you arise and engage your purpose.

Open now your new eyes. The world is here.

Are we complete? Yes.

Adieu. Fare thee well. Thank you.

Shilogh is here?

Shilogh is here, yes. With greetings for you. And your friends. Those who will read your book. To them, also, I bring greetings and welcome them. Ho!

All is well in the forest today. The forest is breathing. Quiet are the nights with activity. Animals. Yes. The owl is here. And yes the eagle and the deer. And the small animals with chirpings and scurryings.

And you are welcome here. To step inside in your meditations. Where trees ruffle the winds and ferns twist on their stems, where, in day, the sunlight comes in pieces between the trees, making quiet on rocks with lichen where you may sit.

In the evening you see the stars above all the spaces and the night air krinkles down to where you are sitting.

Come to the forest often and renew yourself. It is here. To renew you and be renewed. The keepers of the forest keep it ready for you to enjoy.

Bring your energy here and feel it cleansed, refreshed, and, as you leave, give your blessing to the forest.

So it is with all things. A giving and receiving. A knowing you are blessed. An honoring of self and others. This we know is true.
Come often. I invite you. You are welcome here.

And take this moment now to sit underneath a tree and let your eyes close softly. And let yourself be renewed by eternal connection with all that is.

Smell the pine trees. Hear the scurryings and brushings. I am here. I keep you safe. You may drift off into your own knowing.   And later when you come back to here, you will find me, standing, watching all around you and making peace.
So be it. All is well. Ho!

July 14, 1999 afternoon eating grapefruit
For someone

Be easy in your time of trial. And let yourself not be held back. Ready you are to progress and go on. And yet others cling to your garments. They cling *because* they see you leaving, going on ahead. They cling to hold you back, take care of them. And yet, they must learn that you must go on. They must learn what you have learned: You are responsible only unto yourself, unto your innermost knowing. You may not make them your excuses for not honoring your self, your god, your godself, your wisdom. There are no excuses.

Be easy in your trials, knowing this. Knowing the star that you steer by is your star though no one else see it. This will not be understood by explaining. Waste not your energy. For each person, there is a time to come to his/her own knowing. And that time might be any moment. Hold yourself from judging those whose time is not yet. You are a shining example for those who would see you. Those whose eyes are closed must wait to find their example in their own time.

It is your purpose only to be true to yourself. Think how harshly you will deal with yourself if, for any reason, when you meet face to face your godself, you must say, "But…"

This is not an easy path. And yet willingly have you chosen. And in honoring yourself, you are honoring all others.

When you speak with love, your love returns. And you can hear love. And so do you discern that which is love from that which is not love.

Many there are who support you. Know that we are here.

Recognize your misgivings as we recognize them, also. And now is time to let them go. Stay focussed squarely on where you are going, not where you don't want to go. You think this soon will be over. It will not be so soon. Prepare yourself for the long way.

Use not all your strength now. But set the patterns that will sustain you. Nourish yourself. Call for love. The outcome is assured.

Take yourself to the forest this being tells about. And know that you are trusted. Know that you are safe. Wobble not in your course at this time. Keep your sighting on your star.

Adjust. Adjust. But always in your own keeping. It is enough to remind you? We see you and applaud.

Love, Faith, Wisdom.

All is well.

July 14, 1999 evening. Pine Grove. Meditation Circle led by Joyce Orcutt, medium/clairvoyant.

> In meditation, I see Jesus, Mary, Kwan Yin, Great Bear.
> Spirit telling me, letting me know, we like your book.
> Grandpa, grandma stand behind me, one on each side with a hand on each shoulder, proud of me.
>
> Joyce Orcutt confirms:
> Spirit *is* happy with the book. It's to flow like water. Just get out of your way. If there's a hesitancy, just go on because they'll come back to it. Just do what you can and have patience. The book will bring "solace and peace to many – those not only in this land but in other lands."
>
> Patty Nelson, medium/clairvoyant:
> I see you sitting and often Kwan Yin comes in and merges with you. Essence of compassion. I see a book of verse that doesn't go with what you're doing now. So you put it aside.
> Keep putting it aside. It's another book. It will be finished within a 24-month period. I see it in print. I see it in a foreign language, almost, I would say, an Oriental language. It will be a big help to many many people.
> I see a being around you a lot named John. He will be a great help to you.
>
> *I want so much to bring their gift to the world. And I thank you for your reassurance and encouragement and presence. And I thank them for their presence and their patience.*

July 14-15 ~

I am a writer. Spirit speaks through me in words on paper that the words may be remembered.

Those of you here as light workers, creating the spaces and grounding the light into the planet, Know yourselves. Know yourselves through the time of discouragement that it be short, through the time of unbalance that it be balanced, through the time of keeping still, that you inherit great wisdom.

For as you know yourself, greater than your imagination to do so, the energy of your being calls to you what is needed. Fear not. This is so.

We see the lights which are you, sparkling in your worlds. We see the beacons you become as you align with your own greater purpose, highest good. And we rejoice.

Your light is your name. And by your light we know you. And as you allow us to work with you and for you and through you, as you make this choice, so does your light brighten and shine for others.

There is love for each of you to shine your light into dark corners.

Miss not the opportunity to bring brilliance.
Miss not your own brilliance by looking away.
Honor yourself – *you* being here with the purpose you have chosen.
Honor the godself.
And celebrate.
We rejoice in you.

July 15, 1999 chant, writing room

Good morning, dear sweet one.

Good morning.

Last night was good, also, no? (at Pine Grove)

Yes. Last night was very good. Thank you for your messages.

This is our pleasure to you. Important is it for you to know the vastness of your vision. This other book that was mentioned. You know what it is?

Is there verse as in poetry? No. *Just that it's poetic?*

Yes. As is all your writing. You bring messages for the world. Truly was it given when you asked. "You are meant to teach the world." For in your teachings are the steps to take to oneness, wholeness, on this planet. It's why this whole planet responds to your writings. As has been said.

Establish yourself a new place to stand that is on a high place that you may be seen and heard and acknowledged and paid attention. This is the time.

Go forward in the circles you've made and bring the circles with you. Leave not them behind as you step forward in greatness. Now is the time you've been coming to. The time you have set forward. Now will become clear why you have guarded your privacy. Your privacy continues to be important. Spill not out of the container you've made, but pour carefully into places you choose.

Your prosperity also draws closer. Watch for this and watch for opportunity for action.

You know I would shine.

Yes. We know you would shine and so, you do so already. Do not underestimate the effect of your shining. Dreadful, that would be.

You are the hollow flute and more. For in hollowing you contain your essence. And what you are doing now is showing others how to do this. Sing yourself through the flute, for we are listening.

Much love, peace, and gratitude come to you now and through you to others.

July 15, 1999
For someone

This is not the only book you'll write. Stop stalling to keep it close to you. To do it some approved way. Write this book and send it to the universe. Other books are waiting. And people are waiting for this one.

You haven't begun until you've begun. And when you've begun, you have called the finish. Allow the finishing now and get out of your own way that this wisdom come into the places that are seeking this.

If you play the game someone else's way, expect someone else's results. You know how it is to be done and you are the one to do it. Be not led astray by others' promises. Stay true to yourself, and the strength of your purpose carries the result.

Methinks you are looking for money rewards and so withholding your gift. Bring your book to the world as the gift it is. And all prosperity follows.

Much needed is your wisdom in this time. Fill yourself with the writing. Stop chasing other things being hungry.

Only you can write this book and, meanwhile, are we waiting. Much love.

We honor you your vision, your sincerity, and encourage you to move on your dream, which is ready to manifest.

July 15, 1999 (talking to Sharon Massoth on the phone. She gives this message about the book from her guide: "This writing has such depth. This connected piece is exactly what needs to get out.")

July 15-16, 1999
For someone

There is much good in the world because you have done it. There is much love, and much peace and much laughter that would not be without you. Truly have you touched people in gentle loving ways. And this goes on. This doesn't stop. You cannot stop it. Nobody can. You have done what you have come to do and on a grand scale.

Be not discouraged as you watch yourself take apart what you have built. You have built it well; it has done what you intended. It is accomplished. Rejoice.

The words of hope and trust and faith that have caused a bright glimmer for those who read them are for you now. Read the words you have put together from many sources and hear them speak to you. There is comfort here and daring and challenge. It is no small thing you have done and will continue doing.

What if you need something else of you now? What if the universe does? What if in the circle of chasing thoughts or in the still moment of a dream, a new thought is born, Here is where I'm needed?

Time it is for rest now. Quiet rest that you congratulate yourself and bask in your accomplishment.

Nothing you have done has failed. Look clearly. Everything has succeeded to your highest good. And everything has brought you to this place and time of newness.

We bring you great applause. Your light shines across a planet. Truly, this is yours.

And now have you set it up so there is more. Rest, then, and realize in your resting what it is – your next dream – that will next fulfill you. Truly, have you set aside your former expectations.

The way is clear. We guide you and we ease your heart. Let us. You are not alone.

You are a shining example for others. Not only your courage and integrity, but also your very spirit.

Know that you are blessed in every situation you create. And know that you don't imagine we're with you. Verily, we are.

Listen now for the voice in you that knows and will tell you what's next. No matter how simple or grand that may be, take time to honor it. You are using you very wisely. Now is no time to doubt.

If you could see as we see, the sparks of light on this planet where your spirit has gone, you would see it is time to rest and celebrate.

Celebrate. We celebrate you. Much love and angel kisses. You are adored.

Chapter Twelve

Water the earth with your prayers.

July 16, 1999 morning
(Last night dreamed someone singing to children.)
Chant, welcome archangels, bless circle at Pine Grove

I invite a message, especially for this someone

Be brave, dear heart, for all is well. Even when you think it's not, it is. Fear not the dark night, for haven't I put you stars? Fear not the deep waters, for haven't I made you buoyant? Fear not your aloneness, for don't you walk with me? How, then, shall you fear?

What have you come through safely? And is there only a little more. Of what you can do and have done. And do well.

You are a comfort to my people. A blessed rose that brings beauty into hearts that might otherwise not be reached.

Do you think you are here for you? You are here for me. This you have chosen and do you pursue well our purpose.

Little will you learn now by holding little griefs. Let them go. You do not need them. That is done. Snap not yourself back to old patterns when you find you have left for a while the thoughts you mull about. Instead let them go and step into new others waiting here for you.

Long are the times when you suffer. But short the times you spend in joy. Expand the joy, we say, and shorten the suffer.

Awake to the possibility – you, and see what you have been changing. See what you're enabling you to do by leaving what's past behind. Make a list and show your*self* the choices you make now. Which carry you forward to new choices. And new and new.

Break not yourself apart except in a good way – to rearrange what you'll be today and set yourself up for tomorrow. Tomorrow is coming, you know. And you will be here in it.

And bringing to those you can what you choose to bring. Choose now and choose wisely, that later you not regret a moment of what you bring. Only you have the exact word, exact thought, exact gesture, that someone is looking to receive.

In each day, notice who that someone is and follow-through the gesture.

You are very loved. Unto the heavens, are you loved.

And we applaud. Your courage and your daring. Impossible to make a mistake though you tend to forget that.

Go forward now on what you have learned and what you have brought to the world. Think kindly of yourself as you do of others. Find reflection of your beauty in perfect roses. And smile when you see (notice) the thorns.

All is very well with you as in a while you'll notice.

You'll be calling us to thank us. When it is you who are doing the changes and deserve very much of credit.

Be at peace now.

Love yourself as we are loving you.

Adieu. Fare Well. Be loved.

(When I called to deliver this message, the person said, "This morning I asked for a message.")

And is there something for me?

Swimming is for you.

Go. Relax. Enjoy it.

July 16-17, 1999
For someone

Give up the sadness in whatever way is symbolic for you. Let it go. Ask to be lifted and ask Archangel Michael to cut the attachments to your past.

Dear one. You are being tested in ways you don't like. Rarely do we like the tests we call to us. But always we are the ones who call them. And always are we ready for the ones we call to us. We create tests for our learning, for our next step forward. (*We?* Yes. We create steps for our learning here as well and it is each being who calls her own awakening.)

This is not something being given you but something you have called. Accept this and you are halfway there. For when you accept that you have called it, and the energy has responded to your call, you realize you can change the energy and how it serves you. The energy you asked to respond to a certain purpose you set can be asked to respond differently if your purpose has changed.

Does this make sense to you? We are light and vibration. Energy. And energy responds to thoughts.

The energy that you worry about now has served you in some way. Acknowledge this. Find how it served. So then you may release it to serve some other purpose. We will make this clear if you choose.

Energy is stuck here where it has best served you. What is it that you need to know that it be released? Take communion with yourself.

For not by not learning what you are to learn can it be released. You must access your thoughts and call them to you and examine them.

See where there is love and where there is not love. See where there is forgiveness and where there is not forgiveness. See where there is joy and where there is not joy.

And look at your "nots" and see if they have contributed to the knot you hold in your physical being/self. And see if you're ready to release them.

What is the placement of the knot in your physical being telling you about where you've been? For this was created in your past if it manifests in your now.

And you are not your past. See who you really are and you see that this is true. The tests you have set are meant to teach you this.

And so now you set your future with what you call to you today. Do you send love? You call love. Do you send forgiveness? You call forgiveness. Do you send peace? Unconditional peace? Joy?

Acknowledge the past and what it has taught you. Honor yourself in your past and set yourself free, sending unconditional love.

And set forth your future with knowing what you know today.

You can change what you call to you, but not by holding old hurts or sorrows. Only by letting them go.

Be at peace. Be healthy. Be whole. The spiritual you is here.

July 17-18, 1999

Good morning, Shilogh. How is the forest?

The forest is quiet and very dry. More dry than it should be and this is hard on the animals and hard on the plants. You think this has nothing to do with you, but this has to do with you. As are the forests, so is the world. When you have no concern for the forests, your world will not survive.

How can a world exist in itself without care for all her peoples? The small furry ones, the feathered ones. The larger walking ones, the elementals. No. These are not separate though you live in cities and may not see them.

As the forests thrive, so the world thrives. When the animals find no shelter and nourishment, man will find none, either. This has everything to do with you. Think not someone else will take care of this. You must take care of this. You must take care in all you do, not to waste resources and to honor earth. For earth provides the forests.

As earth provides for you. Think not always of yourself first.

You are keepers of the forest.

The forest is dry. Provide, you, the rain of your good thoughts. Call you the rain of your blessings. As you bless the forest, you bring the rain for all things.

Your prayer supports an earth. As you rain your blessing on the trees, the rocks, the plants, the animals are blessed, the earth is blessed, and you are blessed.

Take care of the forest and its people who live there. They need your good intent. And as your blessing falls on others, it falls on you.

It is quiet in the forest and dry. Its peoples are thirsty for love. Make your prayer the prayer of giving thanks.

Thank you for the rain, Great One. Thank you for the rain.
Thank you for the sun, Great One. Thank you for the sun.
Thank you for the moon.
Thank you for the earth.
Thank you for the creatures.
Thank you for the snow.
Thank you for our peace, Great One.
Thank you for your abundance.

And as you think of the next word, say it. Let the prayer become yours as you speak your thanksgiving and blessing on the forest.

Start with the forest and, in looking around, notice what needs your blessing and do not withhold it. What is freely given, returns.

And I thank you for your blessing as I live here as well. And, in turn, I bless your houses and the places where you walk.

Think kindly of yourselves, precious peoples. Think kindly of your earth.

Thank you, Shilogh. Thank you for your prayers.

(He bows Namaste and fades backwards into the forest. I can see places in the forest where the light comes through to the ground past parched leaves. And the leaves on the ground are dry. And the stones. And the animals are still.)

Thank you for reminding us. This, also, is our task.

Water the earth with your prayers. With your blessings. Be at peace.

July 18, 1999 chant

Namaste

The ways of my country are many, and yet all are one. Different ways do not make things separate. Different customs. Merely, they show the uniqueness of divine spirit.

Cloud not your thought with what seems to be, but look you beyond the seeming. For in seeming, you narrow your mind. In looking beyond, you expand it. Why would there not be differences when spirit is creative? Would you want each flower the same? Each bird with no differences? And yet each bird, each flower, no matter the shape, sings its own song to the creator.

Sing your song. Let others sing theirs and what beautiful song arises.

Know you not that angels learn your songs and sing them, too? One may sing the daffodil or one may sing the frog or one may sing what you hummed at work or while you were outside playing.

Sing, then, the song that is yours to sing, that you have chosen. And listen to the others' songs that you may learn them, too.

Listen to the songs of the faeries and of the ferns.

The ways of my peoples are different. They tell you this in their songs. And the songs say, We are one with you. And this is exactly true.

As your fingers are you and not all of you, think of the ones who sing.

Mind expands to inform you, to include you, and to make you whole.

All is well, indeed. Thank you for taking our messages when we bring them. You take them seriously and with much care and so we bring you more. And truly these words will touch the hearts of many as they come through your heart.

Many thanks. Many plaudits for the work you are bringing here.

You are the messenger, don't you see? Hermes. Thoth. Combined and uniquely you.

Without messages I wouldn't be a messenger. Thank you for what I carry and deliver. Thank you from a host of beings as well as from myself. Amen. (Coming back now. Getting soft. And getting into body.)

Oh. Is this the connection for writers? That I tell how it's done through me? To leave footprints that may be followed?

Yes!

My experience necessary so others can follow and do it themselves. Is this it?

Yes! Dear one. *VERY YES.*

I'm laughing that it takes me so long to catch on.

We are laughing, too.

I see them laughing and throwing out those curly party streamers and hooting and hollering, tooting noise-maker horns. And now wearing paper hats. They must be thinking the way I'm thinking, "Finally, she gets it."

All activity stops for a moment as they let me know, They celebrate me and with me. But for them there is no impatience as I imply in the "Finally." Only there is the love and the knowing I will get it and any time will be fine. Do I see this?

Yes. Thank you. (I'm nodding and awed by their trust. The celebration starts up again and now I am softly here. With tears in my eyes, a sob in my chest from loving these wonderful beings.)

July 20, 1999 invoke, chant

Is there a blissing for someone?

Yes. Of course there is a blissing for someone. This attuned one is consistently blessed and draws to her extreme circumstances that she may know this. That she may notice. She is in good hands, in good care, and yet she struggles, trying to make things come out right. She hasn't yet surrendered. Or when she does surrender some thing, then she takes it back to worry it some more. This is not necessary. What she gives into spirit's hands will be taken care of. But perhaps not as *she* wants it. And so she takes it back and looks again and says, Maybe there is some other way. As long as she wants to solve it, we won't interfere. Each time she takes it back, she changes things. She gives up to the highest good at night. At day, she takes it back.

She can change and rearrange things as much as she likes. Always with our blessings.

People won't eat of the bread she offers them when she keeps it tucked under her arm. (I see her holding the loaf of bread tucked under her arm and with her other hand inviting people.) No. She must offer it with both her hands and let it go for us to know she doesn't need it for herself.

All is well with her. She cannot do it wrong. Always she has choices that are hers to make.

We would say to her, Be calm. Carry your calm around you. Like a flotation device, it keeps you buoyant.

Changes come to you and you must deal with them wisely. And always are you guided. What are you holding onto? What is keeping you from something better that awaits you? Search in your soul. Establish your goal, your highest purpose. And test. Is what you hold on to necessary for you to achieve it?

Let your highest purpose guide you – not your earthly emotions, which are fickle and can change.

What are you willing to let go to let your self come through? Ordinary you are not and so must you think out of the ordinary to progress.

These are challenging times made especially for you. To see your self triumph and succeed.

What has been will not hold any more. Change that way of thought and accept a new way of being. All is made ready for you. You will see, but only later, that this is so.

You are doing the right things. And now get out of your way. And offer unto us what you'll allow us to do.

All is extremely well, though in the leap you don't see where you'll land. The landing is assured. The transition as brief as you will allow. And a world alive and waiting. Come now, why don't you? We're ready.

Does she not know how she is blessed? Does she not let herself be assured? (They speak to each other, shaking their heads, and I arrive back here.)

July 21, 1999 chant, invoke

There's one singing down there.
There's one carrying light.
Kumbaya, my lord, Kumbaya.
Kumbaya, my lord, Kumbaya.
Kumbaya, my lord, Kumbaya.
Oh, lord, Kumbaya.
Someone's singing lord, Kumbaya.
Someone's laughing lord, Kumbaya.
Someone's crying lord, Kumbaya.
Someone's dancing, lord, Kumbaya. (folk song)

I feel me in a different space. Ascended masters in a circle. Baby kicking and waving arms on the throne. This makes all of us smile. And I am getting the realization that even here, the child rules and teaches us to smile. Be delighted.

Jesus stands in the circle to my left, but now seats himself in the circle as Kwan Yin stands and steps forward to the center of the circle. She cups her hands and tosses blessings to each one, blowing her breath gentle as she does and when she comes to me, I feel the sparkles and she goes on. And now she dances. In the center of the circle, she places one foot gently, then the other, whirls. She holds her thumb and first finger together as she lifts her head back. The headdress catches the light. I can see the lines of motion where she's been. There is purple color. There is gold. Others stand and enter the circle and dance. And I am dancing, too. Timid, at first. But no one is watching. Where did these ribbons come from? I have ribbons in my hands – or out from my hands, more like it. As I twirl they follow me, put my motion onto the air. Others have ribbons, too. We see where we have been in the ribbons on the air and swirl again. And the ribbons are scarves that match our intention. And the scarves are veils that swirl around us. We dance. The veils flutter a cocoon. And there is music. And each of us sees her own veil and it is beautiful. And beyond it, some form of motion. We are watching our own veils – what they do when we move like this. Like this. Keep whirling to keep their surround.

And now something stops. And we are still. And the veils flutter down with our arms, come to rest, and we can see each other, shining from the dance. And Kwan Yin puts her graceful hands on her hips and looks at each of us in turn and nods.

And now she is seated on her cushion. We are seated. I do not see the veils. There are no ribbons. I'm not sure at all the dance happened.

The baby is sitting up now and watching the center of the circle. I'm not sure the dancing has stopped or if we still are there in the center, whirling in our scarves.

As I look around the circle, I see light around each being, and all the heads are bowed. I bow my head and hear a voice:

"Revel and make magic. You are born to dance and dream. And swirl the veil and also it is yours to sit in sacred circle and see in us who you are. This is yours, for you to keep. In all of your doings."

I feel a tug in my solar plexus and think it is this knowing being placed where I will remember or it will remind me.

Time for equilance, this is titled, I see. I see banners on sticks standing in a glass jar. I set myself adrift.

Softly, I hear birdsong. Chirpings. The paper I hold in my hands is large/full size with golden marbleized edging. There is something printed on it. I hear church bells chiming. I bow Namaste to the bowed heads. I am in my body in the chair. Sounds of traffic and birds.

Bright air comes in at the windows. A car shifts gear and bellows along a cross street.

Thank you. I am blessed.

The sky has feathery clouds. Sounds of the traffic fade into neutral background noise. The curtains flutter.

I get up for tea, see a note on my desk. "What can I do to help you to help me to help the world?" which Al Ferency says at message circle.

Be strong. Be present. Be lifted in the moment. For truly you are a light to the world. The candle was given by someone who notices for *you* to notice and not forget or think you make it up.

Your presence is felt and appreciated. And, as you see, acknowledged.

This world is changing. As some veils go down, others must go up. And so is the beautiful dance. You are rearranging your selves. All needs will be met.

What can I do?…

You are already doing it, don't you see? And causing these changes. Little chance you have of doing something other. This is it. You see it come back in smiles. In appreciation. And yes, we see you would do more. But already are you doing what is needed. You are listening to yourself and you are listening to guidance and don't you find balance in your days? Don't want to work harder when now you have the balance. That would put it out of whack. You hear wisely. You act wisely. Be at peace.

Thank you.

July 22, 1999 chant, invoke

There is something to learn about color. Born are the colors of dreams.

Color enhances the air you breathe. For truly, you breathe in color. When the color is vibrant, the air has good energy, strong energy. When the color is dull, the air has poor energy, weak energy.

Surround yourself with color. Clear, vibrant, color. Calm soothing color, whatever is needed for you in the moment.

Haven't you noticed that what you wear affects your mood, your energy? Each color has vibration. When color matches the vibration you're needing, there is harmony. When not a match, depletion. Your hands can feel the color. Let your hands reach for you the color you're wanting.

In your rooms, color affects your air.

Like music that fills the air, so is color. And at certain times you choose certain music for soothing or energizing, so choose color also to hold you in love, to support confidence or goad you to action.

Experiment with you to find what color you're seeking.

Thoughts come on colors, also. Different vibrations. Note how you respond.

As I meditate

A woman approaches a performer who has just performed with flute. He sits cross-legged on a raised platform in what seems to be a museum room. He has performed in a different room. Now he is at rest. I have the impression he is a Native American from the Andes. Seems to me Incan or Mayan. The woman approaches. He was quite formal, aloof, during his playing, and now he sits with – oh, his knees are up, his arms crossed across them, his hand holding the flute. He still seems unapproachable to me, but the woman apparently knows him, comes to stand in front of him and say, "I want you to teach me what you did in there (performance). I want you to tell me."

He smiles a little archly that she would ask. And then he answers, "I called the colors. It is time for the colors and for you to know about them. And so you can use them like music to align yourself. To quicken and balance your chakras, your meridian flow. What I have done, you can do. Without the flute." He lifts it to show her. It has feathers and colored beads, teal blue, yellow, orange beads. "Call the colors with your voice," he says, "with your dance, with your drum.

"Colors respond to your thoughts and so you build your aura. They respond to your emotions by changing. Little do you know about this now. But I have called the colors. They have come. Use them now for your own results. Colors are like angels. They will help with your intent."

He lifts the flute to his lips. The woman steps back slightly. "I call the colors in on my breath," he says, "and here is how it sounds." He sounds the tone.

"And you stand in the color now," he says. "How does it feel to you?"

"Soft and a little prickly like sparks."

He calls another. They are in a room with some statues and lots of space. The space fills up with color.

"This is what I was doing, is it not?"

"This is it," she says. She has her eyes closed, sways slightly, breathes the colors.

"There is more to learn," he says. "Pay attention. The colors are here."

(Last night I was made honorary queen of the faeries, I remember, at a guided self-healing circle.) The faeries have scintillating colors.

I'm off. When I come back, the woman is seated now. The air is full of sparkle. I am sparkled, too.

Thank you. May I bring the colors here?

You may.

Colors come.
Colors come.
You are welcome here.
Spin yourselves in light.
Spin yourselves in dark.
Colors you are here.

(The colors dance. Like children, like faeries, they sparkle and do handsprings.)

July 22-23, 1999

I'll get up unless there's a message.

You are loved, querida (dear one). Deeply loved. Unto the heavens are you loved. For you are truly an angel to those around you. You notice their needs and you comfort them. What is this but angelhood? What is angelhood but this?

Truly, are you an angel among us. Bringing yourself to engage with matters of the spirit. You fly back and forth from heaven to earth, from earth to heaven in what you are doing. Call this what you will. We call it angel. Yes. The faeries love you. They adore that you do stories. That you help do stories, and are delighted that you record so they can hear them over and over again. If you find the faery tapes played with, it is them. The red wagon is a useful device to bring them here.

Keep writing. *And* do the preparation for your workshops. (I'm studying, writing, preparing to teach a Melchizedek Method workshop, a writing workshop, and four Reiki workshops.)

All this is important and helps each other. It is the same high vibration for both results.

It is not just information, but more in the way of attunement. The way you understand attunement – alignment with divine source energy.

And this is what you pass on in your work, written or workshop. This attunement.

People are ready for this attunement. They seek it, are looking for it. They accept it and make it their own.

You have been chosen for this work. Don't think it would just happen. And you have worked to be chosen. Have worked to clear your field, empty the cup, align your intent and your courage and your patience. We see your diligence and we applaud.

Proud are we to work with you. And eager. Rewarding it is for us to see our thoughts manifest so surely. Our word-thoughts come down so crisply. Thank you, darling angel. We are blessed.

(I doze, see beings with communications, guidance, papers, moving as in a room around me.)

Thank you.

Thank you and good morning.

Shilogh?

I am here. Things have shifted/are shifting. Thoughts can shift a universe. Intention more powerful than you imagine.

When you sing, Thank you for the moon, Grandmother, Thank you for the moon, you are blessing it to shine. The moon knows and notices. Your blessing is no small thing.

And when you bless in advance what isn't here yet, you draw it to manifest.

Bless the things you would have with thank you, as if you have received them.

Make this a part of your day. And watch how your thank you's impress the world to generosity.

Big celebration is happening now for the changes the peoples are making on earth. (He would go, not to miss the celebrations.)

I will come again.

Thank you. Ho.

July 23-24, 1999 ~

You have 7 years to accomplish my work.

July 25, 1999 morning. Waking. And first thing at writing room

The skies will get dark and the thunder will rumble.
And then it will not rain.
Do you a rain dance.
Call the skies. Call the spirit of the rain and make it welcome,
Not with needing but with love.
Not with call to the dry earth
But with invitation, Dear water, we invite you to make us whole.
With the feel of the rain drops on your uplifted face,
With the taste of the rain water on your tongue,

With the bright strike of rain arrows on your chest,
Call the rain.
With the thunder in your voice, call her.
The lightning in your fingers, call her.
Be you refreshed in this rain you call,
And what you don't need, let the mother earth accept for her own makings.
This is called the rain dance
That all creatures and earth be blessed.
Call the rain with appreciation of the bright taste on your body,
The puddles that form in your hands.
Now the skies become dark with thunder.
And on the dry earth there is rain.
Thank you, Great One, for your blessings.
Thank you for your rain.

(Rain after days of heat, humidity, at 1:30 or so afternoon. I dance. I stay out in the beautiful rain until I am well–drenched and cold. When I go inside to take off my wet clothes, the rain stops and the sun comes out.)

July 25, 1999 invoke, chant

> I see the ascended masters in circle, Jesus to my left, the baby sitting up on the throne. Beyond the circle, angels, around the circle in rings around rings, palms together. They are singing. They sing the chant I just finished singing. They carry it on.
> They show me a grand cross of the four directions as if sketched clear on a clear overlay above them. Somehow I know it is there. It is the four directions and the ancient + cross and the grand cross of the coming solstice.
> There is no shadow of this cross, there is only the seeing and knowing it is there. With their singing it shifts slightly in alignment. It seems to take on light. From their singing, I imagine. In the circle, the beings are quiet. They sit with eyes closed, experiencing.

At first I was seeing this as from above. Now I am seated in the circle. Their eyes are closed, but I look up.

The cross seems to take on brightness and then it lifts and tilts and goes spinning off in a direction past the throne.

The singing now is joyous. The ascended masters smile. I feel as if something that was to be accomplished has been accomplished. The rings around rings that the angels were making around the circle are not rings any more but clusters of angels rejoicing. The ascended masters turn their own circle outward and there seems an acknowledgement, appreciation of masters to angels and angels to masters. And this in a quiet way of no words.

Now the angels are receding, fading back from the circle. The ascended masters turn inward. They accept assurance themselves and the feel that I get, once again, is the feel of accomplishment. It was lined up for something to happen and something did and it is well.

CHAPTER THIRTEEN

You make a difference to the world.

July 25, 1999

A meditation:

You are deeply loved. Unto the heavens are you loved.

What is your gift? For each of you brings a gift. Though often you choose not to see it. You choose to wave it away. You can choose to not use it or misuse it or use it with good intent. Even so, it is yours. Your will determines its use. But still is it yours to use.

Sit quietly with yourself and ask that your gift be made known. Ask that your gift be shown to you in ways you understand. And ask how best to use this gift to accomplish the greatest good.

As you acknowledge this gift and as you use it, you may be shown other ways your gift is needed and may be applied.

You are using the gift of the universe and the universe is using your gift. See how this expands you and how you become aware.

And sit in silence with yourself and ask, What other gift do I have? And as it is made known, so you use it and watch it increase.

This is made for your knowing. That your gifts may expand into blessings and your blessings rain down upon you.

All is well in our worlds as in yours. Blessed are you in our keeping. And blessed are we in yours.

As you give thanks for your blessings, pass them on. What is encouraged grows.

July 26, 1999 invoke, chant

You are deeply loved. Unto the heavens are you loved.

Tell the world. It is its time to shine. It is its time to sparkle with the energy of the new millenium. Don't wait. Start now to show your colors. This being works above ground. And so do you. Though you know little of this yet, you will know more. You will know for true and real that you are guided and safe. You will be shown that this is so in no uncertain terms. Why wait? Act now as if what I tell you is so, and so experience it now.

You have, always, your choice. Many of you have chosen in the past to believe not in your own guidance. That belief is changing. Let it change. It is not necessary. It limits you. It gives you excuse. You use the excuse to escape responsibility for your action. "I didn't know. I didn't do right action because I didn't know."

Take away from yourself this excuse. Accept responsibility. Play with this new belief: I have responsibility and I have guidance. This unlimits you. This is freedom.

When you admit at your deepest knowing, that you no longer need excuse, you open the way to the highest good for you. Clear?

The only reason for you not to hear or sense or feel your guidance is to not believe it's there.

When you make the shift to acceptance, you unblock your access to this knowing.

This is not possible when you limit yourself to not being responsible. Responsible *means* being true to your highest good, your limitless self.

So what is it I'm saying.

Don't wait for a new time or date, but make the change in yourself now. The change to what you *think* you will have <u>then</u> is *made* by changing now.

Those of you who release limiting beliefs now, not only experience their guidance, but make the way clear for others to experience theirs as they shift the belief system of a planet.

Think not one person doesn't matter. Get quiet and hear yourself tell you, "You make a difference to the world."

Thank you.

Namaste.

Namaste.

July 26-27, 1999 dreaming asleep

> There's a message on the answering machine. It's Michael. And in the dream I know it's archangel Michael.
> *Thank you for calling. (I say in the dream and wake. Now I ask Michael,) "What may I do for you?"*

Tell my story.

Do I know your story?

I will let you know.

Okay.

> A little at a time. Be aware and it will go together and you will understand it and so will others.

It will be my pleasure.

> Yes. Truly it will be. (I'm seeing Grandma and Grandpa Doo's when I was little and we'd have vanilla wafers and milk.)
> Childhood makes it easy. Yes. What-cannot-be hasn't formed yet. Go into the place before what-cannot-be and hear my story and write it, please. And thank you.

Will you please let me know it is you?

You will know. Or you can ask.

I will do my best.

Thank you. (I muscle test. Is this a being of the highest good? Yes. And is it the being we know as archangel Michael? Yes. I feel spirit touching my nose. Oh, is this angel kisses? Yes.)

Is there anything you wish to communicate now, Michael?

You have been taking (down) my thoughts. It is well.

Do you mean just now or in the book I call journal?

Both. I mean in both.

Some of what has come has come from you?

All. In different manifestations.

St. Germaine, Shilogh? Dreams? These be manifestations of you? Yes.

So I really am getting information from St. Germaine? Yes. *From Shilogh?* Yes. *Who are manifestations of you, Michael?* Yes. *Wild.*

(I sense he's smiling.)

Yes, it is wild, isn't it? Here we go. Hold onto your hats. (This reminds me of a person from another country who has learned English and this particular idiom.)

I <u>am</u> from what you might call a foreign country. Why do you think you spend so much time there in dreams?

Aha! I may still call you Shilogh at times?

Of course. When I am Shilogh.

Thank you, archangel Michael. You are welcome here.

And you are welcome here.

Namaste.

Namaste.

Did I write down that crows woke me so I'd understand I was bringing healing back here from the beautiful place of pink light I was in? This seemed to have to do with Michael. Thank you, dream bringers, for these beautiful dreams.

July 27, 1999 invoke, chant

I invite highest wisdom, highest guidance, to speak with me now.

I attend the circle of ascended masters, am wrapped in their acceptance, love, warmth. I feel more attentive now, as if I can sit up straight, not round into myself. It's okay to be noticed. It's okay for me to be here. I haven't been disruptive yet. (They're laughing.)

Good morning, wise one. We have news for you. Hardly could you be unnoticed. (I think this a compliment until I look down and see me wearing a faery ball gown of net and sparkles. We laugh together now.)

Your gift has been waiting and now you use it wisely. As you use it, you learn more about it. Is it not so?

And this you must tell to others. As you tell them, you don't need to know how the story ends to write the story, tell them, You don't need to know all about your gift in order to use it. As you use it, it reveals itself. Honor the gift, whatever it is. Accept that it is yours. And use it.

Some may have a gift of consoling others. Some may have a gift of joy and laughter. Some may have a gift of sharing bread.

Think not your gift must be written on the skies. This is not usually the way.

Accept the quiet gifts, the kindnesses you do for others and for yourself, the thoughtfulnesses. And watch them become loud, expand. This will be using your gift.

Think not small of yourself. No gift is small, but each important. And without you, your gift is lost.

I see planets, galaxy oriented to the central sun. "To go to Israel at one time, you had to go into one of the signs of the zodiac. This is not so now." I'm being shown a map of this – like a pull-down school map – and at the same time, a 3-D picture with dark space as a background. This has to do with the alignment of where we are (earth) in relation to the great central sun and how that alignment changes. Has to do with new energies coming to earth in the August 11 and the winter solstice shift.

Is this so? Yes.

This is the alignment with the great central sun? Yes.

How will this shift affect people?

When they know their gifts, it will enhance them as it enhances alignment with their selves.

When they do not know their gifts, the shift can cause confusion.

Can it cause harm?

No. Not harm, but a confusion as it does not align with outdated thinking. Those who know themselves as unlimited beings will find the energy empowering. Those who don't will find it confusing. It will still come in, but without ways to accept it.

Do not despair. These beings will be taught and helped along by others until the new way seems the natural way – which, indeed, it is.

We tell you these things now. So they may not be such a surprise. Many great things are happening. Be loving with yourselves.

Think not you must understand all this; merely, know it. (I see this is a big joke they appreciate – as we physical beings spend so much of who we are insisting to understand and miss so much of who we are by not noticing our knowing.)

Suspend your disbelief. We are here. You are in good hands. You are so loved for everything you are – not just some of it.

Be easy with this. Already it takes place around you. Revel. And rejoice.

For it is you bringing earth her changes. You and you and you. Much love. Many endearances.

This is being accomplished.

Thank you. Namaste.

Namaste.

(I open my eyes and am here.)

Correct? Yes. *Complete?* Yes.

July 27-28, 1999

> I let someone who made the transition from the earth plane recently know if he wants to, he can come in. Am shown by motion – fast motion up straight – he's gone to a very high place. Then see yellow flowers on a bushy-type plant. Not a bush but shiny greenery, near a house or building. I don't see the building, just the wall as if looking down on them. Yellow trumpet-shape flowers as if it's one plant.

July 28, 1999 invoke, chant, begin meditation

> I see words being highlighted across a screen. Two lines of printed words, colored highlight in motion. Message is for a woman.

Is it for his wife? Yes.

> Know that you are loved. You are loved beyond asking and beyond doubting. This is yours. Truly is it given. You accept it.
>
> Live your life in the now, though, with it, you keep the memories. Don't miss the now for the memories.
>
> However you construct what is now is appropriate. Remain present.
>
> Your memories are your memories, not your life. You have much to give and are giving much. You have much to accept. Be easy with this. Accept things lightly, that is, wrapped in light.
>
> Sparkle the world around you, as is your wont. Fetter not yourself or others with your expectations or with theirs. Instead, free yourself from expectation, and so free others.
>
> Then will things come to you naturally and then will you let go.
>
> Make each day your own day. Choose. I want this in my day today. Then release and let it come. All is in arrangement as you like it. Struggle not against it. Choose. Release. Accept.
>
> Much love is here for you.
>
> Perhaps you will see the flowers and know what is meant by this. Yellow flowers shaped like trumpets grow near the side of a building. Much love is here for you and much release to your own life. You know

best for you. You know. Trust your knowing. You are good at this. Stop the struggle and trust the knowing and have patience, dear, have patience.

All is well. You are blessed. You are a woman, a strong woman. Aside to me:

Tell her she is loved. She doesn't understand what love is. That love would let her go and still be loved/love.

When she truly understands this, she will know to trust herself, her givings and misgivings, her what she has and what she wants.

Tell her it's all right she doesn't hear me. I am very fine. And I send love. The freeing kind. The kind that says unlimit yourself as I am learning here.

Much love and kisses, angel one.

Thank you. Is it (the person from last night's dream)?

Yes. Watch for the flowers.

(His wife confirms the flowers are yellow lilies in her yard.)

July 28, 1999 meditation

Good morning, loved ones. Good morning, lord Sananda. (I take my seat in the circle.)

You have been doing well, dear one. We applaud. (They do. I'm surprised and pleased.) We wish to adorn you.

Oh, my goodness. They have one of those trophy sort of ribbons that goes around the neck and on it a medal in the shape of the sun with rays. Someone crosses to me and puts it around my neck. It is very large and the medallion falls between my heart and solar plexus.

They seem to be singing or I imagine, "You are my sunshine." Is this real? The medallion is to remind me of them and their applause.

Yes.

Thank you. Thank you very much.

Your applause is coming on earth, as well. But let it not turn your head into playing for applause. What you really need is here. What is there is for you to <u>do</u>. Play not for the applause, but <u>do</u> what connects you to here.
All is well with you and with us.

Thank you for the medallion, for the reminder. Please don't hesitate to show me again or tug on the ribbon or somehow get my attention if it looks as though I'm forgetting. You know my purpose.
I am very touched with your applause and also with your gift. May I give you a song?

I think to sing "You are my sunshine" and am filled with energy chills. I sing.
Energy energy energy. The baby waves a rattle or a sceptre.

Thank you for my sunshine. (I fade back here.)

July 28, 1999 At a meeting to discuss forming a spiritual center:

It is beautiful that you gather. That you see each other and who you are. Fear not the outcome for it is assured. Where you meet is not as important as that you meet.
Gather your energy now and create the space you would draw to you. How can we provide space without your direction?
The coming together is important. Now state your requests, that your space meet all requirements of beauty and other.
You create your space with you.
We create your space with you.
(I see a golden triangle-like shape which looks almost like a temple flame, stylized.)

July 28-29, 1999 dreaming asleep (This person recently left the earth plane. I see her wearing pink.)

She tells her niece she needs her dining room table. It's not that she needs to keep the dining room table (for herself) but that there needs to be an agreement between the giver of the table and the receiver. The person needs to want it. Don't just get rid of it – make sure that it is wanted.

July 29, 1999 sing Namaste, invoke, chant. (Same person from the dream comes in, again wearing pink, soft suit or jacket.)

You're doing a fine job, dear. Keep it up.

Thank you.

(The person who showed me yellow flowers) is here, you know. He's fine. We only saw him once. He's working – not working, but he's on a project. Something he's doing. (Seems up beyond this, I'm sensing.) Something important.

That table's all right, you know. I can let it go. I don't know why I made a fuss, but good to see my niece. Bye. Bye.

Bye. Bye. Thank you for coming.

Oh, that's all right. It's fun.

Shall I tell your niece?

She was there!

Yes, but that it's fun?

Oh, yes. That. (She waves her hand.)

(Her niece says there was serious discussion about the dining room table which then went to someone for whom it has meaning.)

CHAPTER FOURTEEN

Remember who you are.

July 29, 1999 (Cracking sound as of something coming in behind me. I look and see the angels on the bookcase. Oh, yes. I invite the angels, angelic realm, archangels, especially Michael who sent me roses. Energy chills.)

I invite spirit to use my words to bring a message to those who are waiting.

You are tired of waiting. You are waiting for things to change. Bring about the change. The change comes from within you. Change that comes from without you is merely reaction.

Your change is well-intentioned. Bring it into being. Put your waiting to good use in bringing change, and then it is waiting no more but intention and calling and action.

Your groups that gather intensify energy to this purpose. Worthy it is that you do so.

Water the earth. She is dry. She is parched. Water the earth with your blessing of coming together, intending change.

Supply nourishment for her peoples with the highest intention of showing love – shining love all around you.

This is for you to do. This is for you to do now.

Creation is ready for you to stop waiting and do this service.

Belittle not your gifts and your shinings. You are blessed. Cause blessing to fall upon others that this is so/be so.

Remember who you are. Accept your power. You are ready to use it in delightful ways. Ways that enhance your world, and make it bright.

Step out of your self – your self that your self says you are – and into your magnificent being.

Don't angels gather where you are and add their light to yours? You are much very loved. So be it. Adieu.

Thank you. Namaste.

And thank *you*. Namaste. (This is someone speaking Michael.)

July 29, 1999 meditation

Not using common sense. Using invisible sense. (Someone touches my left cheek.)

> I keep coming back to help with something – when Christ has performed his Iraqi thing alone.
> There seems a rocking chair, wooden, in the center of the writing room. Smaller than ones we have. Afghan or shawl? in it. It rocks gently – facing west (behind me as I face the corner). I don't see anyone in it. And then Jesus is there, holds the what-may-be-a pillow in his lap and rests. He puts his head back and closes his eyes and rests. I've made a good space for resting, it seems. He may stay though I move around, we indicate to each other and I start to be present here pulling white light with me. Fully present in form.
> "Inform." Hmmm.

July 29-30, 1999 ~
Someone from the spirit world tells me:

> He is very loved, this child, in ways he doesn't think of. He doesn't always know what love is. It's just maybe a word. And so he sets up ways to find out and more is finding out. It isn't easy but is working, sort of.
> The work you're doing brings in love and brings in light and so the environment can't help but lighten and this is good. You see the changes. This being has been hurt and so is hesitant to respond.

Each response, then, is great growth. The giving and the caring he gives is showing this. It has not always been so in a way as free as this. This now, is being a helpmate as was intended. (A hood or cover – I'm shown – is being let back cautiously.) The caring without expected response. This is new. He is learning from his own self now and letting go ways he learned very young.

Brightness. There is a brightness here. People are learning new ways to be. And he is one of them.

I think I missed one thought while writing another. Can you make it clear?

(I see a six-pointed star – the merging of the male and female natures? Masculine feminine?)

Yes. That's it. More coming into balance. In a way he can accept. This is big and can be celebrated.

Paths or pathways that have been blocked – no access – are coming undone. That is, the blocks are coming undone. And so we start over. He is very loved. Like a baby, is he loved. And you do your part for it is a big part to play.

Thank you. Did I get it how you want it? No.
Is there something to change? Yes.
Can you tell me?

"Melt." The hardness is melting. The cold is melting. Be sure to notice. (Image of ice cube.)

Is this it? Yes.
That I'm to notice? Yes.
And that it's okay for me, too? Yes.
Do I have the message now? Yes.
Thank you. (I see her with a hat on. A flat sort of tam toward the left side of her head.)

July 30, 1999 I sing *"How Great Thou Art."* I remember Grandpa, then Grandma, at Pine Grove. (They appeared behind me in spirit in the message circle led by Joyce Orcutt, July 14.) I cry, invoke, chant.

Someone cares about you. Someone does very much caring. Accept it for your own, this being loved.

Try not to put it aside as if it can't be for you. When you but accept this, you turn on this light for others.

You are missing something by not being present. Be present. Be presented with what is for you. And so can you present to others what is for them.

Give nourishment where nourishment is needed and so you take care of others.

Turn all your assets to good purpose. The one you wrestle is you. Give in to your highest wisdom, your highest good, and so serve yourself and others.

Stop talking yourself out of this, allowing doubts and fears. Doubts and fears are merely you limiting you. Set them outside your self and allow the truth of your knowing. By this are you held guided. By this are you held safe. By this are you grounded and lifted in your true purpose. Revel. Celebrate. This is so.

Relax into the arms that hold you. For from relaxing into love, do you blossom forth. Already have you begun this, but sometimes you hold back and catch yourself lest you fall.

These arms are the arms of divine mother holding her child. Be held. Be brilliant. All is well with us and with you.

Thank you. Namaste.

Thank you. Namaste.

Is Shilogh here?

Shilogh is here with greetings to you. Much have you been loved and much love is coming to you.

Love has become, with you peoples, a word for song, a word used for rhyme. And so has lost some meaning.

It is about to get some back. It is about to re-emerge as peoples empower it with new meaning.

It is meant as heart connection which is also connection to soul. Watch for this to have meaning in all around you.

You have been taught that love is for people when you know there is more than that. There is love for animals and trees and rocks and ocean and love for a sunlit day or a feeling in that day.

Unlimit your word of love. And yet, use it wisely. Use it not without true meaning, for by that does it erode.

There is something you mean to each other that is more than this word conveys. Watch for the meaning. Watch for the word. Watch for how you use it.

The word is of a physical world and you be beyond the worldly. This is what it means to dance. This is what it means to sing. Connection with beyond-the-worldly.

Sing yourself to that place and dance yourself to that place. You will feel the word I mean and you will know.

> He steps from the edge of the forest with a rattle made from a gourd. He dances, beats the earth with his feet. He shakes the rattle. He sings, lifts his face to the skies in chanting. He whirls and dances and chants. I see he is showing love to the earth, to the heavens, accepting love.
>
> What we call love – beyond love – communion. Appreciation. Honor. What he dances.
>
> I am silent and then I dance.
>
> I dance with the beat of my feet.
>
> I dance with love in my hands.
>
> I dance.
>
> And when my feet turn to shufflings and stop, I honor Shilogh. Thank you.
>
> And my body fills with energy chills as if someone is holding me.
>
> Shilogh is smiling, also, shakes his rattle at me and turning, is gone in the forest.
>
> And here I am to tell you.

July 30-31, 1999 awake but dreaming Pine Grove

> Al Ferency looks at me and says, "Spirit is ready to speak and you're helping." Before this he saw me on some stairs – saw the light around me that is spirit.

July 31, 1999 I sing *"We gather together..."* chant, invoke

Today might be a rest for Randeane.

Would you speak?

We would speak. For this is resting, isn't it? Resting in the assurance of your clear connection. Yea, verily. It is.

You know me.

We know you. You would rather do this than not do this even when you think to take a day off. At the end of that day, had you not written this, you would be restless.

Restless. Yes. I see. That is it, exactly.

So now we begin. What would you know?

I would know something that people are wanting for their own peace and comfort.

They already have peace and comfort, you know. But they knock it aside. They knock it aside with looking at what others have and they don't. Or what others don't have and they do. They look at others as if others have come in to learn the same thing as themselves and so compare. This is nonconstructive. This puts limitations as it calls in fears and envies, disappointments, uncertainties.

We would tell them, Set aside all this. Give something else for your thoughts to work on. Give something for your thoughts to create.

Each has come in with his own things to learn. Others call what is theirs to learn. Concern not yourself about them.

And see what is yours to see, what is yours to create. Create for yourself what you need and what you want. Focus your self on your self. Provide for you.

And here comes the peace. Here comes the comfort. And you find it spills over onto others.

Fill your cup by pouring into your cup – not by looking away at others' cups. Pouring while looking at others' cups, you miss your cup, and it is empty.

Now find the peace is already here. The comfort is already here. Within your own self is it here and you just have to look to see it.

Let others have a fine time with what they're here to create. And you have a fine time, too.

Thank you. Namaste. It is a comfort.

Yes. Namaste.

July 31-August 1, 1999 dreaming asleep

> Grandpa George briefly sits on a chair in front of me. Hat in his hand dangles down from his knee.

~ awake – This poem comes

When Grandpa died

I see him at the foot of a tree. Grandpa.
Kneeling, with the saw turned off.
With his head bowed.
-As they've told me he was-

The tree is a young straight tree that soars upwards.
The tree calls him.
He sets aside the saw.
His being shoots up the length of the tree,
Bursts into green leaves and keeps going.
Leaving here, at the base of a tree,
A form of where he's been.

Grandpa wraps himself around me.
I am 5 years old.
He guards my nights, my days.
And now am I grown?
Am I strong enough for him to go home?

Grandpa wraps around me.
I tell him I am strong.
Thank you, grandpa.
Thank you, many years.
I watch while he goes home.
And cry the tears I didn't know how to cry at 5.
Thank you, Many Years, thank you.

Grandpa sits where I may see him and shows me he's fine, holds his hat down over his knee.
In a straight-backed chair against the wall in sunshine with sunshine coming in.

August 1, 1999 nap dreaming asleep

Kwan Yin comes and sits. I am on a mountain top with chill mist around, blowing past. All is gray. Then below there is light, a golden light that illuminates a golden city with towers. Curtains blow gently in doorways. Many-colored curtains with gold patterned borders. The air is full of light and festive. The people have light brown skin and smile with happiness. If they hurry, it is for the fun of it.
On the mountain top, Kwan Yin holds up a string of beads. I see the bright city through Kwan Yin, seated. And yet now I am also me, standing facing Kwan Yin, the bright city behind and below me. Kwan Yin puts the beads around my neck twice. I am small compared to her. I sit with my back against Kwan Yin's legs as she sits cross-legged, and I try to look regal, as she does, overlooking the city that we protect and bless.

Waking

"This is my divine consciousness tree. It is yours to nurture." I'm shown a tree that twists upward and has horizontal branches out from the top. "For you to know me and me to know you."

August 2, 1999 Sing guides, invoke, chant

I invite highest good to speak through me with a message for the world.

You have changed things and are changing things. You light workers, dedicated ones. Pure is the energy flowing through you to all beings, and to earth, who are in need of exactly this.

Think not that you don't count, don't make a difference. You do.

The light you light within your space carries on to others. And soon are there lights around the earth. And from these lights do others light their own, and there is brightness.

And what we're seeing now is many lights and increased brightness.

The grids provide light where it's called for. And your intent calls it. And so is a connection made with energy. And so is your very form enhanced with light and are you lightened.

Is it not true that others see you lightened and want this for themselves? And so increase their own awareness from having noticed yours?

The energy you are ready for comes to you. Prepare you to accept it. And to shine it forth. It will not be kept still. It will not be confined.

Shine your light in your actions, not in trying to convince. Shine your light and let others see if they want it for themselves.

Brilliant are you and will you be and others will respond and find resonance in their hearts and know that it can change things.

When you work to highest good, highest good manifests, in, of, and around you. It presents others with a question. A question is good and fruitful. A question is not telling or trying to convince, but asking, How about me?

And always is it the asking that invites the change. Be you a light to the world – as you are, my dears, as you are – and watch with joy the brightness that grows around you and more.

Brightnesses, we are speaking to you of accepting your purpose and thriving with it all around you.

Blessed ones, light beings.

(goosebumps. And tears, real crying, as this connects.)

August 3, 1999

Sit.

Perhaps rest?

Ha. Ha. Ha. Do you want a message?

Yes. Of course, I want a message. Yes, please.

Know that you are blessed.

I am beginning to know.

Know deeply, full-heartedly. Don't be afraid to know. Knowing is accepting, a way of saying thank you instead of pushing it aside. Like a compliment, no? You accept the compliment and feel glad or you push it aside, feel unworthy, embarrassed, non-accepting.

So we say, don't push it aside. This knowing you are blessed. But know it, accept it. The blessing is truly given and wishing to be received.

Thank you. I know I am blessed. I appreciate I am blessed. I thank you that I am blessed.

How could you pass this to others if it were not so?

Oh. And I would miss that, indeed. Truly am I blessed.

Get out of your own way again and again and again. It is your only practice. Truly are you loved. We remind you, and it is safe to do this. Step aside. For when you step aside from hearing worldly chatter in all sorts of devious forms, then can you hear the universe and the world. The chatter would take you from hearing what you have to say.

People fill themselves with noises and wonder why they don't hear. Step aside and engage self with your own self and not with man-made other. And then will you hear the richness of thought of earth and skies.

Tame are your imaginings when tied to your man-made clutter. Clear out. Clear out. And empty the cup that the cup may be made full.

Is there anything you're wishing to ask today?

Is there?

You're wanting us to tell you what you wish to know?

Yes. Please.

You wish to know that all is safe for the 2000 year transition. Know it is. Changes are being made. What people may be expecting need not happen with dire consequences. The changes of consciousness on your world are changing this.

The entire dimension is changing toward light, raising its vibration, dropping density. But perceptions are changing also so this may not be obvious. What is obvious is a brightness we've mentioned, a recognition of worth.

Not in any false sense, but in a sense that is true. Accepting that you are truly blessed is a recognition of worth. And why this is so important. And why we want you to know.

Times were we couldn't tell you. And times were you couldn't listen. And now is a time we may tell you and a time you may hear.

Think, already, then, what a change this is and a result of the changes you're making.

Is there something more? Yes.

Don't forget to dance.
Dance down the sunshine to you.
Dance forth the rain.
Dance that you hear things in your sleep and the flowers happen.
Dance the dance of the hummingbird sipping sweet nectar.
Dance yourself connected so you feel the earth and touch the skies and paint the rainbow.
Dance to feel the love beams shining off from you.
Dance to feel the love beams shining into you.
Dance until you see them, hear them. Dance until you know they are there.
Even when you sit still.

Show yourself this is so.

> I chant. I dance. I experience rainbow sparkles. The lines of light I see remind me of the divine tree in my dream. And suddenly, I know, I am the divine tree. And the lines are sparkles of light all around me. And I am blessed.

(Afterword: this sounds quite tame when I read it, but was vast in the experience. I say, Dance yourself to know. "Show yourself this is so.")

Shilogh?

Yes. I'm here. I love the dance. You show the world your heartbeat when you Dance. You show the universe. Your connection in god.

Truly are we beings blessed to have a heartbeat that resounds our song. Our own song of knowing and unknowing. Mystery.

As you give wonder to the hummingbird, so the creatures of nature give wonder to you when you dance your song.

Be not covered in your branches, but shake them forth around you. Spread them out and let them sparkle. (When the Trees Are Laughing) You are loved. We will tell you until you are sure.

And the heavens applaud your dancing, see your spirit shine.

You are the tree, mighty warrior of peace. And so do you trees connect heaven and earth and shine in their presence.

(I'm seeing a lightning bolt grounded by a tree and the tree is not damaged, but rather sparkles with light as of tiny faery lights.)

This that you see is coming. The bringing of energy to earth in ways not this extreme, but ways that make you sparkle.

And now I must dance.

> He does and I see trails of sparkles as he whirls, hear snappings as he stamps. He makes alive the space he is in. The animals come and watch.
>
> He dances himself lighter.
>
> And lighter. I see through him.
>
> And now I see the sparkles of where he has been.
>
> The snappings move off like a thunderstorm gone by.
>
> A hummingbird sips air where he's been and rises on the spiral.

CHAPTER FIFTEEN

Stand in your greatness.

August 4, 1999 chant

Thank you for your wisdom, lords. Thank you for this love that begins me where the tears start.
Cry me and shape me into futures that are waiting to come. (I start crying as I feel the presence.)

You are doing well, wise one. Do not mind the crying hard that tells you how loved you are, that softens what needs to be softened so you understand.

Love is not brittle, you know. Why be brittle with love? Allow the tears that change your face out of patterns, that help your breath sob in this feeling, that help your heart break open and allow.

It is not too big for you to wear though it sometimes seems overwhelming.

Stand tall. Stand in your greatness. Would you not be replenished with love that you give to others? Would you not be filled, sturdy one, with all that you can hold?

There. The tears have stopped and you are shining. Mind not the tears that are your truth, your worth, your glory. The weeping is not sad. And it is welcome, is it not? As often we come on tears and so you know us for who we are.

The brightness we have spoken about is a brightness in vibration. A quickening of holy mind. What you call it doesn't matter. You divine beings are in the shift of energies. Are you surprised that you've prepared yourselves for this and it comes? This vibration of love you can hold and you can ground to mother earth and she can hold it, also. Open your eyes and see that this is so.

You have done the preparation. Be not surprised that it comes.

Spread your branches and feel the sparkle all around you and wear it well that others feel it, too.

Breathe it well that you fill yourself and lift. And lift Gaia with you. She is ready, too.

There are the tears stilled completely, for you have something to do and are doing it.

And for this are you praised. That you choose to wake up and simply be.

Aware

In form

Informed

Information processors for worlds beyond worlds.

Love holders beyond time and space.

Great beings of love and light.

We salute you and applaud.

We would have you know certainty and forget doubt.

We would have you know courage and forget fear.

We would have you know fullness and forget hunger.

We would have you know yourselves, your enchanting, magical selves who are creating this new thought-world. And peopling it with yourselves.

Thank you. Ho!

Ho! You're welcome.

August 5, 1999 I sing "Let there be peace on earth and let it begin with me...," invoke, chant

Blessed angels, you are welcome here.

We feel your welcome. We hear you welcome us. And we come. Bringing gifts of light. And love. And energy.

For isn't this what is needed? As the heavens open, there will be some who see us, yes, and others who know we are there. Look up. The heavens are all around you. Look up that you may not be looking down with eyes closed to see us.

The attitude of lifted head and soaring thought invites us. Though, also, you have known us to come when you are down-hearted and need liftment.

Revel now in the results of change you bring. Pass quickly through your doubts, your fears, for they are no longer needed. And leave them behind as you step forward into shining raiment. Be as we are, full of lightness. It is charming, we assure you. And much will you be loved and loving of yourself. Much will you be honored.

And the need for others honoring you will pass when the love makes you this full.

Truly have you experienced the conditions you have set. And when you're ready, step aside. Let us wrap you in essence's cloak that you experience the lightness of being.

Still the thought-forms around you and sit with us for a while. And we will make you cozy. And we will make you loved.
(Sit quietly with eyes closed.)

And when you know what we say is true, come back, refreshed. And know you can come again.

Message for anyone?

For someone. She still is wanting Peace. To forgive herself. And step out of her own way.

Call and let her know you love her and that we are thinking of her. Or write. Yes. That will be fine. She doesn't have to struggle. She can put the struggle down.

August 5, 1999 (I go to Rebecca's, meet Rebecca's mother, Deborah. Working beyond time and space, we determine, through muscle testing, that I'm an ambassador for peace and that this book teaches "the language of the culture of peace.")

August 6, 1999 (I'm all energy sparkles and crying as I write "Peace ambassador" and think to sing "Let there be peace on earth…" Hear, "You asked." I did ask, "Let it begin with me" – more energy sparkles. I sing and understand when we are at peace with ourselves, we are at peace with the world. That's what "Let it begin with me" means. And I am teaching inner peace.)

Yes.

Thank you.

I ask to be a vehicle for your divine love in this and many universes. Thank you.
Is there a message?

Of course, there's a message. We are so happy you will take it, that we may give it to you.

Yes. This is your work. For you are an ambassador of peace. And love. Which are the same, are they not?

For when you love yourself, without condition and without constraint/restraint, then are you in harmony. And in harmony is peace.

I am seeing people in a hall where I am speaking. This is in a foreign country. I am saying, please stop. And everyone who has been talking is quiet.
I give instruction how to build the golden holographic sphere around the room. I have each person connect with another's heart on the golden thread between them.
This is what is important. This is what they take home and so influence others.
The energy stays around the room, around each person.

Yes. This is it. For when there is peace with oneself, there is peace with others. This is it entirely. This book is being written as a guide to peace with oneself. (I feel a tug in solar plexus.)

It may be that as we complete the work/play for this book, you begin taking notes for the next.
When you're ready…

When you're ready...

Have you said what you'd like in this book? Yes and no.
Is there more? Yes.
For today? Yes.

The kindness you do for the faery creatures is a kindness for the world and all peoples. It is noticed and applauded. Yes, we know that isn't why you did it. We applaud why you did it, which shows the attitude we are talking about. (I invited faeries home with me when their woodland spot was cleared.) The "them is us" attitude, as replacing the "them and us" outworn way of thinking.

Get down on your knees on the grass and feel your experience from there. The grass will not mind and what you will do is reawaken your perspective. Be a tree and be a rock and be a flower, a bird, a faery. Breathe in the nature of things. Grow in the sunlight. Allow your edges to soften and unfold your inner heart to the knowings of trees as harmony, the rocks.

Perfect harmony in themselves. And remember.

Come home to the harmony within you. Kneel in that place. Stand in that place. Act in that place. Speak in that place that your words be truly spoken.

You are loved.

And, therefore, love yourself.

From this, all else follows.

Thank you.

August 7, 1999 chant, invoke
(The circle surrounds me and I am with the holy masters.)

Everything is well with you and with us. And so, you have found out a higher purpose. And how do you like it?

I like it. Thank you.

Truly is it said/given unto you, "You are chosen. But you have worked hard to be chosen." (in a dream July 23-24, 1999) And know you, that what you have accomplished is enough. Nothing more is needed.

You tend to think what more? What more? When you think of things in that plane. And yet we would have you know, if you sit down today, or curl up under the blanket, already have you done enough and that would be perfectly fine. (They're laughing and I'm laughing because we *know* that if I sit down, I write, and if I sleep, I dream.)

Yes. We know you will do more, want to do more, but also it is for you to know this is your choice. Already are you celebrated and adored.

Thank you.

We will help, of course, in what you have planned. Already are we helping. (They lean forward in the circle toward me to indicate they're working for me, for this project.)

All you plan will succeed. Don't limit what you plan. Your thoughts carry forth the pictures and so you create. Your words carry forth your intentions and so you create. You step aside when appropriate and so we create.

We are a good team together, no? And all of us are blessed. (Look who we have working with us, they point. And the one they point to is me. It makes me smiling happy and I know that later I'll know the exact thing to say at this time – but I also know, that in this circle that reads hearts, I won't have to have said it.)

Let's go, I affirm. Let's keep going with this wonderful creation, leading people home. (I see a dream from March 99 in which I'm leading beings upwards into light.)

The ascended masters stand and all hold glasses for wine and give a toast to the new project and the completion of the book. And silently, I toast them – and feel by the energy sparkles, that they know.

Thank you, Great friends. And more. Namaste.

Namaste, sweet one. Many kindnesses for you. (They stand with their glasses raised and as I come here, they sip. This is solemn, though full of lightness. I am full of sparkles.)

*Words flat on the page do not convey the deep awe and emotion which accompany much of this work.

August 8, 1999

Good morning, dear ones. I thank you for all the energy, all the love, all the light. I thank you for my great role in this experience. (Goosebumps big time.)

(Then I invoke and chant.)

Good morning to you.

Good morning.

We are pleased to be here, hear you sing. We laugh, though, that you hold your nose.

Yes, you made me laugh, too. It's a technique.

Yes, for looking funny.

Thanks.

We joke with you, but we *like* the song, your voice, your breath, which reaches us and calls us. Use the song as a blessing, yes. For we will bless those where you call.

This sound is your call. For us. As each has its own call. The deer, the elephant, the magpie. Each. Its call is its connection. Its invitation. This is so.

Make friends with the sounds around you, for they are others' call. And you will hear as we hear, the spirit of each call. Mock not any one of the calls for each call is important.

Hear the call of the leaves and the grasses, the song of the tree. That each emits a frequency that is known. And we respond to.

Could you hear as we hear, you would think your world a noisy place, indeed.

Has this to do with the song of the daffodil I heard in a dream? And chanting of the chickens?

Yes. You were hearing their songs. This is it exactly.

Be aware, even when you don't hear, that each being has its song. Hard it is to mistreat others when you hear their songs.

Your world has mostly stopped listening or covered up the noises with noises humans create.

If humans were listening for their own song, this would not be so. Still yourself and hear us come, quietly, to your call.

Bask in the loveliness of our offering. (I feel the lovingness surround me.)

August 9, 1999 invoke, chant

Any messages?

For someone

Take it easy. All will be accomplished. Take not onto yourself that which you cannot handle gracefully. All is well. You hold loving space and energy for those around you. This is enough and more than enough. No wonder people notice you in special ways. Appreciate what you're doing as we do, also, appreciate.

What is it you would give away? Give away. It will be fine. You'll see. Keep for yourself what it is you need and what it is you want. And let the other go.

Suffer not over giving away what is yours to give. Many times does it come back to you, your giving.

Be easy in your work and in your play. For in your living, do you set an example for others. That they may know how to act with love and with contentment.

(Pause and change of focus.)

Truly are you meant to teach the world, Randeane. Haven't we been showing you this? When you ask, we answer.

Yes. Thank you. Is there more?

There is more and more and more. You think you have arrived somewhere because now you think you know where you're going. But truly, you have just begun. Finish this book and the next has already started.

Finish this trip and the next is already planned. You are needed. (Here I am crying again.) You are wanted. And you are willing, is it not so?

Yes, dears. I am willing. I am thrilled.

And we are thrilled with you. This is very exciting. Make your plans in pictures that you then step into. Hurl them out ahead of you for when 3rd dimensional time gets there. And let us enhance them a bit, if you agree, as we're in the pictures also.

Yes. Let's enhance them for highest good and thoroughly enjoy.

The healing bubbles you saw on the hill slope can be created anywhere. We add them now to whatever pictures you create. (This was in a dream.)

We see them as bubbles around you, also, in pictures *we* create. This is a mission of light, dear. Be comfortable all the way.

Thank you. Thank you. Is this Namaste?

This is Namaste, bright star, with all our loving wishes.

August 10, 1999 invoke, chant

Yes, we're here. How are you?

I'm starting to think of camp and school and feel some pressure of time.

You don't need to, you know. You are outside time and everything is accomplished. As you step outside constraints of time, you free the path for things to happen, come to fruition. Easy it is to wrap yourself in time and so create confinement. It is a natural thing to do where you are, where clocks create time and people believe it. And their belief gives it strength.

But you step through the doorway and see/understand the vastness around you and know that time is a convention only, to try to break vastness into small enough pieces to comprehend.

It is artificial, then, that has become natural for you. It is not from nature, though, that goes in cycles and feels the winds, that basks in rain when it's rainy, and basks in sun when it's not.

Be you like the trees that know when to pull up juices for green leaves and when to let leaves fall and rest.

This has been a heart time, a time of producing green leaves, and yet there is a rest time, too, that you may bask and rest.

All is already accomplished. You need just to fill in the form (of it) to bring to manifestation what already is.

Rest yourself. And then take time to complete. For already you've started something new. Nothing is lost by resting. And everything is gained.

Timing always completes itself in your world with or without watches. Be present and be aware.

Thank you lovely beings for being all around me.

(I go to an evening drum circle. In a recent dream, spirit came to me and invited me to dance. I was told that I dance with spirit so others may walk. And so, at the drum circle, I dance.)

August 11, 1999 invoke, chant
Shilogh is here

I see you dance. There are many people and still you dance like a warrior, like one made for dancing. This is so.

Leaps will be nice, next time. You are a leaper. Think on this. One who leaps into and one who leaps over and one who lands well; flies well and grounds well. This is no coincidence, no accident. That as you leap, light one, the wind carries you. As you lift away from mother earth, spirit arranges your direction. And when you land, you ground the flight into mother earth.

Think of the peoples of many realms who receive, then, from mother earth. As we adjust your flight and attune your landing, you bring this good to earth.

Next time, leaping then, to indicate this is so. Mother shifts a little while you're up. And you shift her with your landing.

All is lightning around you. All is thunder. And here comes the rain.

Thank you, Shilogh.

Ho.

CHAPTER SIXTEEN

You are not alone.
What you long for is here.

August 12, 1999

Is there a message?

Yes. There's a message of hope. Did you want to invoke? (I invoke.)
There is a message of peace.
There is a message of love.

Long have you human kind given yourself struggles and misunderstandings. Now is a way made clear for new understandings on many levels. For long have you had wisdom but not understood it. Long have you had grace but not accepted it.

Now as you invite wisdom and grace, you find it is already here waiting to be discovered and waiting to be used. Children of the earth mother, realize who you are. Accept and welcome home the tools that are yours to use, the guidance that is yours to guide.

Weary are you of not knowing things you think that you might know.

Still yourself and commune with yourself and set your star path on your highest purpose that you may accomplish it and be glad.

For in this time is each one needed to uplift the earth and all her children. And why are you here if not to take part in this glorious undertaking. Come, we invite you, and use your gifts, and prosper yourself and others.

What think you will be the outcome if everyone sits aside for someone else to take action? Act on your dream, your deepest soul purpose, the reason you have come here.

Invite us to help. We love to be invited and will help in ways we can.
Learn from all, that you teach you. For, truly, you teach yourself well.

Let us be together often in the thinning of the veils between the worlds.

We leave you with a blessing. But we don't leave. Where you invite us, we stay.

Thank you.

Thank you.
Namaste, we say at the same time and we bow.

August 13, 1999 chant

Gather all the sparkles of brilliance from around you and draw them into your chest, into your heart center. All the brilliance you emit, coming now, back to center. Feel it gather. Feel it spiral and converge in pure light.

This is for you. Renew yourself and sit with yourself in quiet and step into the silence.

And when, in the silence of your own heart center, you know you are truly loved and truly cherished, when you feel the smile on your lips that this is so, let yourself expand, that your light extend to others, and step back softly on your way.

Do this often in your day, we urge, a few moments at a time, and watch the change. (I feel a buzzy touch below my lower lip through this.)

I see me at a lecture hall. I am inviting the angels, the higher beings to be with us, and I say:

And at this time, you invite, also, those who are your angels, your guides, your higher spirits and selves to be with us and bless this time together.
I chant.

I see white light of source and hear "and be with god."

You are doing well, tall one. You are doing well. Rest now for more will be coming to you – that you will love. And so, now rest, and be at peace. For this is totally awesome! (I'm laughing out loud at his choice of words.)

Thank you, sir. I'll rest.

> I invoke and find myself in the white light of god. I smile. *Here I am again.*
> So I see. (He caresses the holograms with his hands, turns me around as if to say, "Scoot," and tells me, "Rest." And I am here.)

August 17, 1999 camp, morning

> Sometimes I see Shilogh at the edge of the forest, a beautiful man manifest in feathers and simple clothing. He sits today on his horse, his feet hung down loosely past her sides, relaxed. He sits still, as if he has waited, and greets me when I come. Good morning. Early peace.

Good morning. Early peace.

I like this place you have come to rest. The lake, the trees, the light, the bird twitter.

Even the mirror sings here, and the breeze brushes off (away) the head fog. Good it is to be restful and quiet and fill with the solace of nature. When you allow it, nature soothes you. And makes you her own. In rhythm and balance.

You are her family, but you forget and needs must be reminded. How close we are in god.

Do you feel the power in what you are doing? Bringing yourselves home?

Thank you, Shilogh.

There is such power in resting.

August 19, 1999 invoke, meditation at camp

As we stand around you, we see your glow, the lamp which is you, calling people to your light. We are proud of your progress, dear one. In resting, you allow the progress you've made to catch up to you and recharge you for the next stint. Truly are you well-directed, well-intentioned, and the beams you shed do provide guidance for those who are seeking.

Each must find her own way else risk being led.

Enjoy the trees, the lake, the moon and stars, put here for your enjoyment. Draw in the energy. And next year come two weeks.

Thank you.

Namaste.

Namaste. (In them, a circle around me, I see the white light of me reflected, and from this, see the white light of me.) *Thank you.*

August 21-22, 1999 dreaming asleep

"Carry with you always." I have a backpack of useful information.
If I carry it with me, I'll have it for any circumstance.

August 22, 1999 Back at writing room, invoke, chant, meditate
Shilogh

Welcome back. And you had a good rest-off. And now you are renewed by the pine trees and the lake and the island. Eager to get started on what is next.

Well, eager, yes, but still feeling soft and drifty.

Soft and drifty is good. Enter gradually the things you left here to step into. Nothing is a rush just now. Move kindly through the things you do. As each takes order, you advise and allow and be carried. Be lifted and aware. All goes well. In our worlds and in yours.

Thank you, Shilogh. Namaste.

Namaste, my friend.

> After this, I have a new cup of tea beside me on the table. I turn
> to making notes on dreams from last night. As I notice and
> note that the man who showed me yellow flowers in a dream
> was at a wedding with his family even though he's in the spirit
> world, I turn to lift my tea cup and am startled full of energy
> sparkles as I see that a feather which had been across the table
> on a thank-you note is balanced across the top of my tea cup.
> The windows are closed. The fan is not on.
> I did not move the feather. I am quite impressed and delighted.
> I sing as a gift for this lovely gift. And I don't get over it. Every
> time I remember, I smile.

*When I tell her about this, the woman who sent me the thank-you
note and the feather says that, yes, that was a feather she'd picked up,
thinking it was a gift of beauty sent from this man in the world of spirit.

August 23, 1999 chant, invoke

How may I help you to help me to help the world?

Just by being present. By being aware. By recognizing and
acknowledging the energies/light beings around you, you allow them/
us to do much good. All is well, truly well, and, as the veil thins, you will
see this.

Remind each other all is well. Be curious about the next good things,
not waiting for what could befall you, but creating, with your dreams
and imaginings, much beauty.

Truly are you blessed in your creating. Be fulfilled. In all your longings.
You are not alone. What you long for is here. Turn and recognize it.

August 26, 1999 chant, invoke, meditation. Message as I come back.

Any message?
For someone

Be sturdy. All is well. Each day changes you and you change each day. Much progress is being made even where progress is not visible. Allow it to enfold you as you unfold it. All is well. And cheery.

Sacrifice is not necessary to be loved. You are loved. You are appreciated. Revel in this. Be the goddess that you are. (Here I see book or books – as in read about goddesses.) Look upon the goddesse and see she is you. Her attributes, her attitudes, you.

There is much here unexplained and unexplainable. You are safe. Even in the unexplained. Be sturdy in accepting your self that is your glorious self.

You will not be confined. You expand beyond limitation. All is well. Rejoice. In quiet calm.

Is there more?

For you as well. Rejoice in quiet calm. For all is yours already. Things shift as they will. And what you thought was there may not be. And so shift with things to new unlimitations. All is very well and you are in charge. Maintain your momentum – your rhythm. For much is accomplished in the quiet waves of your being. And much there is to be.

We are pleased to be with you.

And I, with you, also. Thank you.

And now you begin your day?

Which is already begun with you. Namaste. Thank you.

Namaste. (We bow.)

Thank you for being ever-present, that when I step outside of time to greet you, you are there. Thank you for helping me to help others. I am truly blessed. And thank you for finding me the times to meet you as I begin a new/old schedule – teaching at the college.

August 27, 1999 invoke, chant

And is there a message?

Of course, there is a message. We have been waiting (while I do invocation, chant, cleansing meditation).

Sounds are important to you. And it is because sounds carry vibration or vibration carries sounds. They come together and you perceive the sound which signifies the vibration.

Sounds come at times to bring your attention to something of notice. Their meaning is clear to you. When there is no perceived "cause" for the sound, it comes as affirmation of your thought or knowing, as punctuation of its importance.

There is much to know about sounds which manifest in your dimension, and also, that sound from your dimension manifests as vibration in other dimensions.

The words and tone and volume of your singing/chanting register here as vibration of love and call to you your service. As you request, so bursts forth to your dimension the avenue of your seeking. Have you not noticed that when you call, you are answered.

It is no accident what is coming to you to do. For you have called it forth from the higher dimensions where it is heard, "I am ready."

Greet yourself with love, with understanding. This is so.

As you state your willingness to serve, your path of serving comes. Be careful, then, with these, your energies of sound. Be aware at many levels. For even as you hear the sounds we make to you, we hear the sounds you make to us.

All is well and truly given. Be at peace with this, which is yours to know.

Thank you. Namaste.

Namaste. Thank *you.*

August 28, 1999

Are there any messages?

There is a message of hope, peace, and goodwill. Often is it misunderstood that goodwill resides at home.

Good will is thought to mean doing unto others when in truth it is doing unto self. For whatever is the attitude of self unto self will be the attitude of self unto others.

From you cannot shine a light to others that does not shine in you. If, then, you would extend good will to others, harbor it at home in yourself.

This shows wisdom, peace, understanding. Focus on this for its meaning. Still yourself and be alert. Hear and see what it has to tell you.

In listening, much is given.

August 29, 1999

Is there a message?

Yes. There is a message of good will. Limit not yourself and others by thinking small. Of only those you know or those you like. Everyone is needing good will. Your Santa Claus knows this when he wishes Merry Christmas to all and to all a good night.

But you tend to picture "nice people" when you think of good will. Instead think of all people, past and present and to come and you will expand your vision, unlimit your scope. This is fruitful. How will it be when all are included in blessings? How will it be on this planet and beyond? Check with yourself if this is true. Go into the quiet and hear.

August 30-31, 1999

Is there a message?

You are loved beyond thinking. True it is what someone said last night. You are deeply healing, deeply spiritual. Hesitate not to tell others. They are waiting/wanting to know. All is well. You are doing this fine.

The book is still here and still coming. Work/play on it as you can. Always is it coming. You will find as these others (books) begin, you find a good place to end with this and gain closure that opens other doors.

Thank you.

Namaste.

Namaste.

September 5, 1999 writing room invoke, chant, meditate
(I am in the circle of masters. The light is peach-colored. The masters sit cross-legged. Sananda stands in the circle to my left.)

You have a new project. The other is done/complete. When you put it together, you will see how perfectly it completes itself.

The new one is one you have already begun. In fact, it is more than one – several. This tiny being (Katherine) has been waiting patiently to see her words in print. She is eager and all are eager to have her project proceed. Also there are dreams and there are verses – as you have been shown. Put them together in books that others may hear and see the marvelous things that come through you.

We are not impatient. We see this proceed apace. The other work you do also is healing the world.

This is for you now. To take joy in the completion. And joy in the new beginning. All is well with you in all you do and don't do.

Shilogh is here to speak. (I see him stand with Sananda, first in leggings only, but blossoming into full regalia with headdress and beads and moccasins.)

Ho! I would be with you.

You are welcome here.

And wherever you go.

Yes. Please. Wherever I go.

For you have far to go and have made the first steps of the journey. The journey that will take you to far places. Now are you begun. You have your knapsack/medicine bag/tote that you always carry with you. This was given in dreamland and goes with you where you go. In it is all you need. You need carry nothing else and still will you be sustained and guided and served. Yes. For we would serve you well who have the same intents as yours. We would serve you silently and with loud noises. And gently, sometimes, with words.

You are our bright star. And we follow you. As we also guide or lead.

Let there be light among your goings and your comings. And let there be laughter and joy. For solemn we are not at times. And be you not too solemn. The river. The river. Carry me.

Thank you, Shilogh. Ho.
Thank you, Sananda.

All is well. Go in peace. Be merry. Celebrate your gifts.

Namaste, dear ones.

Namaste.

> There is a shining in the circle. I see the door to this writing room open and Sananda step in. I seem lifted on the light and find me here, hearing, "The colors in my hands are songs."

Give yourself permission.

Maybe you're reading this book and saying, "I hear things like that." "I didn't know messages could be so short." "I didn't know messages were so personal. Or so normal."

You might be saying, "Why would guidance want to talk to me?" Your higher self or guides or angels want to talk to you, but you need to give permission. On some level, you need to ask. It is a condition of the universe that energies must have your permission to come into your presence. That's how you're sure they don't come interfering uninvited. So ask for the highest guidance available to you and make known your conditions. As you begin, imagine yourself surrounded in light.

You might state:

"I am a being of light and choose to hear only the words of those who work for me with me and through me for my highest good and the highest good of the collective and of dear Mother Earth. I accept only those of the highest good into my presence."

Once you've stated your intention, your call goes out and you are heard. If your belief admits of lesser energies and you feel you've drawn energies other than those for your highest good, it doesn't mean you have negative energy. It means they are attracted to your light.

This may be a signal to your awareness that you are listening to the part of yourself that doubts and would have you believe this isn't real or can't happen. Turn your focus to it. State with clear conviction,

"I am listening now to my highest guidance," and you'll feel the energy shift to highest guidance.

Any time you sense energy you do not wish to work with, state firmly, "You do not have permission to be in my energy field. Leave now. I accept only those for my highest good. All others I bless and send away with love." As you state your conditions other energies withdraw.

You have authority in your energy field. You are in control and can close a connection at any time by stating, "I now close this engagement and give thanks to those beings who work for me, with me, and through me," and return to full waking consciousness.

Providing a setting

Throughout the book, I've referred to what I'm doing when messages come. Here's some description and suggestion for creating your own setting. Use what works for you, leave out what doesn't, modify and add to create your own invitation.

Dance

If you're moved to dance, dance. It opens and stimulates the energy pathways. We're in body to appreciate the marvelous things it can do, not to ignore it.

Chant

A chant is any repetitive vocal sound. For me chant is really singing. I started by chanting on one note and when that got boring, I played with different notes and now sing the Karuna Reiki symbols. You don't have to have a good voice to chant or sing. I chant in the car driving to work as a blessing for the day and everyone I encounter.

Don't underestimate the power of voice. When you sound your voice, the universe answers. Sarah Benson tells us our singing nourishes the angels. And it nourishes us, as well. Use your voice and keep singing as long as it feels good. When the song sings you, you know you're there.

When I've chanted leading workshops, people have seen angels and heard more than one voice singing.

Invoke

You can invite the bringers of dreams, angelic realms, mother/father god, Great Being, Source. I invite beings of light for my highest good and the highest good of the collective. An invocation conveys, "Here I am. I'll be still for a minute, open to receive."

I'll give you an invocation you might use to start. As you use it, allow it to change to your own words and meaning. It doesn't have to be the same wording each day. Go with whatever comes to you. Your invocation signals/sends the message, "You're invited and I'll be still."

Meditate

In meditation, you **do** what in invocation you intend you will. Be still. Open to receive. If you find yourself thinking about what you might be doing if you weren't doing this, or something you're concerned about, let your self know you're on vacation from thinking. Allow your mind to play. When you're engaged in the thoughts you always think, you won't notice insights or new awareness.

Let the problem-solving part of you that talks to your self – commenting, judging, advising, fitting experience into beliefs – take a rest. Assure that thinking part that you'll give your attention to it after meditation.

Write it down

Often words come to me as I'm sitting in meditation or between sleeping and waking at night or while I'm walking or taking a bath. I write them so I can see again what the message was.

When it's written, meaning that isn't apparent at first is often quite apparent in a quiet moment next week.

As you read, as you meditate, as you allow yourself to notice in thoughts, imaginings, feelings, your own experience of the numinous, the form beyond form, if you write it down, you will have your own journal to assure yourself this is real.

Whatever you think you're imagining, write down.

Whatever you think you're making up, write down.

Imagination and making-up are the allowance, the permission, the paying attention into further realms.

Don't feel you have to "keep a notebook." Write on whatever is handy and date it. Keep your writings in a particular place – a basket, a folder, a drawer.

What happens in dreams, write down. What happens in meditation, write down. If it comes to you in two words, write them down. If it comes to you in pictures, write them down. If it comes as a poem or story, write it down. If it doesn't make sense, write it down. You are acknowledging and inviting more.

The most spectacular things in our lives – the things we'll remember forever, are covered by what happens the next day and we forget them until someone reminds us and we say, "How could I have forgotten that?"

There is no one and only way messages come. Be aware of the unexpected and write it down. What you notice and note can act as guidance. What you don't note is lost. Take a look at your notes every now and then. Learn to look for guidance and see how you notice it. You'll see where you've been and where you've come, you'll see it really happened, you'll remind yourself what to remember forever. You are deeply loved.

Come Back

Before closing your ritual, express your appreciation to guides, higher self, those beings who have been with you. Sincere appreciation is welcome in other realms as it is in this.

Bring yourself gently back to the room. Don't leap into other activities, but enter them gently, softly, with presence.

If you feel a bit spacey after meditation, rub the bottoms of your feet, drink water, eat something, walk outside. You can also ground yourself by extending imaginary roots from the bottoms of your feet deep into Mother Earth.

Setting up your own ritual

You'll develop your own ritual, but knowing how easy it is not to start because "I don't know how," I give you a model to get started. You may want to add to your invocation Kwan Yin, Sananda, the Great White Brotherhood of Light, anyone else who has meaning for you.

Create a sacred space

Sit comfortably where and when you won't be disturbed. Turn off the telephone if you can or choose a time it won't ring. You may not think you're getting anywhere in meditation until the phone rings and your whole self jolts back into your body fast enough to make your heart thud. Better to avoid this if you can.

Sit in a chair with your feet on the ground and with your arms and legs uncrossed. Meditation works in many different postures. I'm giving you one that works for getting started. Once you're comfortable, find what else works for you. I **can** meditate lying down, but usually fall asleep, so if my intent is to meditate rather than nap, I do it seated.

You might visualize or imagine a sphere of golden or white light surrounding you and the space around you. This sphere holds the energy you call in and does not allow lesser energies within it. State your intention to accept only those for your highest good and send others away with love. You may ask your guides, your ministering angels, to keep you protected and safe. If you know Reiki or other symbols, you might intend the symbols into the space you've created with light. This is not necessary, but a good use of symbols if you know them.

Chant if you like

You can chant "Aum" or any symbols you know. You can sing a hymn or make up a song or anything – drumming songs, songs from childhood.

State your invocation out loud or in your head

"I invite mother/father god, Great Being. I invoke those of the angelic realms and those beings of light who work for my highest good and the highest good of the collective.

"I do this for the learning and highest good of myself and others.

"And I thank you for the work you do with me, for me, and through me."

Meditate

You might begin to breathe a little more deeply than you normally would, noticing the breath out and the breath in, releasing any concerns, any thoughts, any tensions on the breath out, and bringing fresh clear energy on the breath in.

When you feel yourself shift into stillness, or if you don't feel the shift, imagine it – this is what meditation is – you might propose a topic or you might hear a topic or a word. Or invite a message by saying out loud or in your head, "Any message for me now?" "Thank you for the help I will give today," or "How may I help you to help me to help the world?" or any other intention which seems appropriate.

And then stay quiet for a few minutes with the intention of listening. When you do this heartfelt and pay attention, something happens. You may feel a tingling or energy sparkles. You may feel a touch on the cheek or on the hand or become aware of that feeling of someone else in the room.

You may sense a slight breeze where there is none. You may feel none of these and, if you don't, you are still in meditation. You may notice your face has relaxed and you're smiling.

Write it down

When you hear something, write it exactly as you hear it. When you see something, describe it exactly as you see it. Don't interpret and then write. Don't judge and then write. Don't determine whether or not you like it and then write.

Write it as it comes, without thinking, opening your eyes only enough to see the page if you need to. Stay in the space you've created and put down on paper your experience. You'll have time in normal waking consciousness to see what it means to you.

Write it down word for word as you receive it. If it's too fast, ask that it come to you more slowly. If you can't get every word, take notes, but don't add your own words or interpretation. If you see colors, write down the colors. Or write how you feel. We are so creative that if we don't write it immediately, we change it to fit preconceived paradigms. What doesn't make sense at the time may be meaningful as you expand your beliefs and trust your authority.

Bring your awareness back to the room

When your attention drifts back to the room and your surroundings, close with your expression of appreciation. "Thank you" is fine. I sometimes close with the word, "Namaste," to show respect.

Bring yourself gently back to the room. Begin to notice your fingers and move them. Let them dance. Notice the chair holding you. Become aware of any sounds inside or outside the room. Not too quickly, bring yourself to the awareness of the space around you, where you are, and when you're ready, gently open your eyes.

You may want to look around the room and see everything anew. Sometimes it sparkles.

If you didn't write down your experience before you came back, write it now. If you think nothing happened, write how it felt. "I saw colors," or "I felt calm" or "I'll do this again. It was pleasant."

When you feel centered in your body and grounded on earth, set a time to meditate again.

Now that you're back in the world, come into your normal activities gently, bringing with you whatever quiet or calm or insight you've experienced.

Allow the learning

When you get a chance to read what you've written, read it without judgment, looking for what it may teach you. If the message makes sense in your wake-a-day world, act on it. If you wrote, "Sit down. Put your feet up. All is well," I'd suggest you sit down, put your feet up, and allow all to be well. Acting on a message you've received shows you appreciate it and appreciation opens the pathway for more.

If the message doesn't make sense or goes against your nature, wait for it to make sense, allow that you may have missed some of it. Ask for clarity in the next meditation. We are responsible for our actions, whether or not we feel we're guided to them.

People ask me, "Doesn't this take all day? By the time you do this invocation and that meditation and write it down?"

It can take you all day…if that's what you want. And maybe some days are best spent in prayer and thanksgiving and meditation and song.

I rather think, however, we "go to the mountain" to return to the earth refreshed and to bring to the earth the presence of our being and to ground in the earth the light that we are.

You may set aside a half-hour or so as you're getting started. As you get accustomed to this, add time if you have it and are out there flying, or do a five-minute version if you don't have the time.

Summary

Sit comfortably
Chant or sing
Read or make up your invocation
Meditate
Write down anything you've noticed
Close by giving thanks
Come back gently

This is just a guide, a suggestion to help you get started. Use what works for you. If you find yourself invoking before you chant or skipping parts entirely, you're setting up your ritual. Follow it.

If you set this aside, saying, "Well, that works for her, but wouldn't work for me," you are taking something away from yourself to attribute to me. But I give it back, knowing that when you're ready, you'll see possibility. And that's all it takes.

Award-winning short story collections

by Randeane Tetu

Merle's and Marilyn's Mink Ranch   *$9.00*   ISBN 0-918949-17-3

"*Merle's and Marilyn's Mink Ranch* is an astounding work of fiction which evokes all of the charm and magic of contemporary New England."   — *The New England Review of Books*

Flying Horses, Secret Souls   *$11.95*   ISBN 1-57601-020-1

"...when Tetu weaves language, mystery, and desire together, as in 'Depth of Field,' ...the reader enters a dream world as encompassing and peaceful as a field on a summer's night."
                    — *Library Journal*

Ordering instructions: (*this page may be photocopied*)

1. Please send your order with a US check or money order payable to:

   Rowan Lake Publishers, 204 Westbrook Road, Essex, CT 06426

2. For additional information, visit our website, **www.rowanlakepublishers.com**

Select the following (list number of copies and multiply by book price)

_____ **When the Trees Are Laughing** @ $14.95 each	=	$ _____
_____ **Merle's and Marilyn's Mink Ranch** @ $9.00 each	=	$ _____
_____ **Flying Horses, Secret Souls** @ $11.95 each	=	$ _____
Sub total (add dollar amount of books ordered)	=	$ _____
Sales tax (Connecticut residents only, add 6% of sub total)	=	$ _____
Add shipping, $3.50 for one book via USPS	=	$ _____
Add $1.00 for each additional book sent to same location	=	$ _____
TOTAL (add sub total, tax and S&H)	=	$ _____

Please mail my book order to me at:

Name _____

Address _____

City _____ State _____ Zip _____

Telephone (____) _____-_____ E-mail _____

ROWAN LAKE PUBLISHERS
204 Westbrook Road, Essex, CT 06426